Fun, Facts and Records

Higher . . . bigger . . . further . . . but records have to be looked at in the light of other achievements as well. Did you know that the flea is the world high jump champion? It jumps nearly 20 cm/ 8 inches in the air, which doesn't sound very much. In fact, that is 130 times the flea's height. If a man could jump 130 times his height he could hop over St Paul's Cathedral (149 meters/ 489 feet) with plenty of room to spare. Yet even the best high jumper in the world cannot clear 2.5 meters/ 8 feet. There are many records and comparisons which are a bit unusual. Do you know, for example:
– How many real jumbos you can get into a Jumbo Jet?
– If a boy can jump 1 meter/3 feet high on earth, how high can he jump on the moon?
You'll find the answers to these questions and many others in this book. Sometimes there is not enough room on a double page to cover a whole topic, but the index on pages 124 and 125 will help you find more information elsewhere in the book. Have fun!

© Copyright 1988 Inter Verlag Koln
English Language Edition designed and produced by Autumn Publishing Ltd, Chichester, England

This 1989 edition published by Derrydale Books,
225 Park Avenue South, New York,
New York 10003

Typeset by Words & Spaces, Hampshire, England
Printed in Czechoslovakia

ISBN 0-517-69601-0

How quickly does

Hair which is 6 meters/20 feet long is a physical impossibility. Even if she had used the best hair restorers on the market, lonely Rapunzel, locked up in her tower, would not really have been able to grow her hair that long. Also, the prince would have had to wait years before he could climb up the plait.

Once upon a time there was a beautiful maiden who was locked in a room at the top of a tower by a wicked witch. The maiden was called Rapunzel. The tower was 6 meters/20 feet high, with steep walls without a single foothold, all around. If it hadn't been for her wonderfully long hair, she would certainly have starved in her prison. Rapunzel's hair was so long and thick that she could easily pull up a basket full of delicious things to eat, on the end of it. The prince who saved her used this long plait of hair to climb up and rescue her from that gloomy stronghold.

Grimm's fairytale is a fairly unlikely story. If the tower had been 6 meters/20 feet high, Rapunzel's hair must also have been at least 6 meters/20 feet long – longer, in fact, as plaiting would make it shorter. Even if Rapunzel's hair had been been 4 cm/1½ inches long when she was born, it would still have had to grow at least 5.96 meters/19½ feet before, say, her sixteenth birthday. Sixteen years = 5840 days. So her hair would have had to grow 596 cm/235 inches in 5840 days, which is roughly 1 mm/ 0.039 inch per day. On average, hair grows only about 0.4 mm/0.0156 inch per day, which means it would have taken 14,900 days – or 40 years – for Rapunzel to grow her hair 6 meters/20 feet long. However, we are talking about a fairytale and *anything* can happen in fairytales!

The woman with the longest hair in Germany, Georgia Sebranke, had hair which wasn't even 3 meters/10 feet long when she was 40 years of age, so it was less than half the length necessary to climb up into Rapunzel's tower. In fact, hair rarely grows for as long as 40 years. Most hair falls out after four years of growth.

hair grow?

The hair of Diane Witt of the USA measured 3 meters/10 feet in 1988. It was 16 years since she last cut her hair.

Some people have more hair than others, quite apart from those who are bald. Blond people have the most hair, with roughly 140,000 individual hairs on their heads. Redheads have the least, with only 88,000. People with black or brown hair have about the same amount – 109,000 and 102,000 individual hairs, long or short.

Some parts of the body are hairier than others. Well, that's obvious! We have a lot of hair on our heads, but it is fairly sparse on our arms and legs.
And yet:

Some babies are born without hair. But even they had hair once – in their mother's womb. All babies are covered in a downy hair which is almost colorless. This hair is not very long, 0.1–1 cm/0.04–0.39 inch, and it falls out before birth. When a baby is born, the hair on its head is much stronger and has a distinctive color and is much longer, between 1–2 cm/½–1 inch. A child has less body hair than an adult, but still has a great deal. The eyebrows alone contain 600 individual hairs, and eyelashes have 420.

Humans lose about 90 hairs per day but most of them grow again. The hair on our head grows roughly 0.4 mm/0.01 inch per day. It grows faster in the morning and in the summer. It does not grow at all at night and growth is slower in winter.

How much hair actually grows on an adult human's skin?

Individual hairs	cm²/in²
Head (crown)	300–320/1935–2065
Head (forehead and back of head)	200–240/1290–1548
Chin	44/283
Pubic Hair	30–35/194–226
Arm (top of forearm)	24/155
Back of hand	18/116
Beard	25/160

How long do the individual hairs last?

- Head – about 4 years
- Beard – 10–12 years
- Other parts of the body – about 4½ years
- Eyelashes – 3–5 months

How fast do fingernails and toenails grow?

	m/inches
Fingernails:	0.86/0.0033
Toenails:	0.04/0.0015
Big toenails:	0.06/0.0023

How long does it take for nails to grow 1 mm/0.039 inch?

Thumbnail:	nearly 9 days
Left middle finger:	7 days
Left ring finger:	10 days
Left little finger:	12 days
Left big toe:	more than 14 days

If nails are not cut, normally they will not grow longer than 10–14 cm/4–5½ inches, but occasionally they can grow as long as 1.50 meters/5 feet.

Fingernails grow less than 1mm/0.039 inch per day.

Fingernails and toenails vary not only in size but in thickness. The nails on the little fingers are thinnest: only 0.35–0.4 mm/0.001–0.015 inch thick. The nails on the middle fingers and toes are 0.41–0.46 mm/0.016–0.018 inch, and on the thumbs and big toes are 0.62–0.65 mm/0.024–0.025 inch thick. Altogether, fingernails and toenails weigh about 35 g/1 oz and represent about 0.05 per cent of a person's total body weight. Every day a human grows about 0.11 mg of nail, and in a lifetime (80 years), that is 300 g/10½, which is roughly the weight of two medium apples. Nails grow more slowly in winter than in summer; faster on the right hand than on the left, and more quickly on fingers than on toes.

Blond people have the most hair and redheads have the least.

How do you transport 18

A Boeing 747-230B (better known as a Jumbo Jet) weighs 352 tonnes fully laden and can take off with 500 passengers or 72.3 tonnes of freight. That corresponds to the weight of 18 fully-grown elephants. The Jumbo Jet is the biggest airliner in the world. It is more than 70 meters/1230 feet long, and has a wingspan of nearly 60 meters/197 feet.

But the **Saturn V rockets**, which were sent to the moon for the American Apollo and Skylab space programs, are even bigger. Saturn V is a three-stage rocket with a length of 110.85 meters/1363 feet. It is twice as high as the Leaning Tower of Pisa (55 meters/180 feet) but not quite as high as St Paul's Cathedral (149 meters/488 feet). At take-off, this rocket weighs about 3000 tonnes and is as heavy as 8.4 Jumbo Jets. Even so, it can only carry 2 tonnes more than a Jumbo can (74 tonnes in all). The extra weight is about equal to one baby elephant.

The smallest airplane in the world, **Baby Bird**, was built by an American, Donald R. Stits, and was flown in 1984 for the first time by another American, Harold Wember. The wingspan of the airplane (1.9 meters/6 feet) is roughly the same as one of the engines of a Jumbo Jet (a turbo jet engine with a diameter of about 2.4 meters/8 feet).

How long and how wide are scheduled aircraft?

Aircraft type	Wingspan m/ft	Length m/ft	No. of passengers
Concorde	25.56/84	62.1/204	144
Airbus A-300 B4	44.84/147	53.62/176	345
Boeing 747-230 B (Jumbo)	59.64/196	70.51/231	500
Iljuschin Il-86	48.06/157	59.54/195	350
Lockheed Tristar	47.34/155	50.05/164	300
Mc-Donnell Douglas	50.41/165	55.5/182	380

How big are rockets?

	Height m/ft	Weight tonnes
Four-stage rocket Titan 111E/Centaur (USA)	48.7/159	620
Three-stage rocket Saturn V (USA)	110/360	3890
Three-stage rocket Ariane (Europe)	47.39/155	200

In contrast, the Hindenburg was a Zeppelin which was 245 meters/803 feet long, weighed 200 tonnes and had a payload of 126 tonnes. A crew of 50 looked after 50 passengers.

The American three-stage rocket Saturn V, used on the Apollo and Skylab space programs, is 110 meters/360 feet high and weighs about 3000 tonnes.

The Saturn V rocket is only 39 meters/128 feet shorter than the dome of St Paul's Cathedral. Even so, a rocket like this cannot carry a great deal – only about the same as a Jumbo Jet.

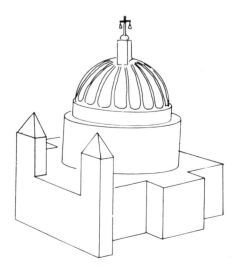

Space and aircraft

A Boeing 747-230 B, or Jumbo Jet, has a maximum take-off weight of 352 tonnes, which is roughly the weight of 88 elephants. When fully laden it can carry 72.3 tonnes, or 18 elephants and one baby elephant.

Rockets are used for space travel and for military purposes. Rockets which travel very long distances are mostly multi-stage rockets. A rocket such as Saturn V (shown in the drawing on page 8) has room for astronauts or cargo in the top section. Under this section, there are three more sections which fire one after another, giving the rocket the thrust it needs.

When do the sections of a rocket fire? Imagine a four-stage rocket which is going to put a satellite into orbit around the earth. The first section ignites on the ground at take-off, and the second section when the rocket reaches an altitude of 45 km/28 miles. The first section is jettisoned and usually falls back into the sea. At 90 km/55 miles the third section fires and the second falls back into the sea. At 550 km/345 miles the fourth and final section fires, the satellite goes into orbit and the third section is jettisoned. The fourth section is up to 18 meters/159 feet long and is big enough for a complete space laboratory. In a three-stage rocket of the type used for manned space flights, the command module containing the astronauts is in the top part of the rocket. This command module is the only part which must return safely to earth.

How big are single-engine aircraft?			
Aircraft type	Length m/ft	Wingspan m/ft	Seating capacity
Cessna 152	7.34/24	10.11/33	2
Cessna 207 Skywagon	9.68/32	10.92/36	8
Piper PA-38 (Tomahawk)	7.04/23	10.36/34	2
Piper Turbo Lance	8.81/29	10/33	6
Baby Bird	3.35/11	1.91/6	1
Piper PA (largest model airplane)	3.44/11	5.4/18	–
Delta (smallest remote-controlled model airplane)	620 mm/24	375 mm/15	–

Where does the sun shine most?

Thunderclouds can be up to 30 km/19 miles long and can discharge up to 20,000 flashes of lightning.

The mountains of Norway have a particularly heavy rain/snowfall: 196 cm/76½ inches per year. But the wettest place on earth is in Columbia, which has 1177 cm/463 inches of rain per year. It hardly ever rains or snows in Santiago in Chile – only about 36 cm/21 inches per year. And probably the driest place on earth is the Atacama Desert in Chile – it hasn't rained there for 400 years.

Cumulonimbus (storm clouds)

The weather is determined by many different circumstances – wind, cloud, air pressure, humidity, temperature, solar radiation, rainfall and visibility. A meteorologist (a scientist whose work involves studying and forecasting the weather) has to observe and measure these eight factors very carefully before he can make an accurate weather forecast. A forecast given 24 hours in advance is correct about 88 per cent of the time, and one given 48 hours ahead is still likely to be right 85 per cent of the time. But a forecast given six days in advance has only a 65 per cent chance of being accurate. There are many weather stations where the rainfall, temperature and hours of sunshine per day are measured. These measurements, and information gathered from satellite pictures of the earth, enable the weather forecasters to predict what is likely to happen.

Where is the sunniest place in the world?

Land which is a long way from the sea is often dry, because sea winds do not carry their moisture far in-land. So the summers are hotter and the winters colder in the middle of a continent than they are on the coast. The highest temperature ever recorded was 57.7°C in the Sahara Desert – hot enough to fry an egg on the sand! On average, the sun shines for more than 97 per cent of the year in the eastern Sahara. This is more than 4300 hours. In 1917, temperatures of more than 48.9°C were recorded on 43 consecutive days in Death Valley, California. In 1969, 768 consecutive sunny days were recorded at St Petersburg, in Florida, USA. The place with least sunshine is the North Pole, and the coldest temperature ever recorded was –89.2°C in Antarctica, in 1983.

The same rain falls millions of times.
The sun heats water from seas and rivers, and tiny drops of moisture rise into the air. As the warm air rises, it cools, and the

moisture droplets fuse and turn into millions of larger water drops, which join together to form clouds. As the air gets colder, the drops become bigger until they are too heavy to stay in the air and they fall to the earth as rain. If it is very cold, the water drops form ice crystals which fall as snow.

You can tell what the weather will be like from the clouds. If you are out for the day on a long walk or a trip to the seaside, the clouds will show you if the weather is changing and it's time to go home.

Weather

Different kinds of clouds form at different heights. They are known as low, middle, and high clouds. Imagine a building with different floors. On the ground floor are the low clouds, which stretch from a few meters/feet to 2 km/1 mile above the ground. The low clouds are cumulus, cumulonimbus, stratocumulus and stratus. They are made up of water droplets, and their temperatures range from 0°–10°C. On the first floor, 2–7 km/1–4 miles above the ground, are the middle clouds, nimbostratus, altostratus and altocumulus. These clouds are made up of both water droplets and ice, with temperatures between –10°C and –30°C. On the top floor, 7–13 km/4–7 miles above the earth, are the high clouds which consist mostly of ice. These are cirrus, cirrocumulus and cirrostratus, and they have temperatures of –30°C to –60°C. But clouds may be found even higher than this. They can spread upwards and outwards almost without limit.

Cumulonimbus (rain clouds). These are huge clouds piled up on each other in a heap. They can be anything from a few hundred meters/feet to 2000 meters/6500 feet above ground, and up to 10 km/6 miles high. If they are dark and gray at the bottom, heavy rain or even thunder is on the way.

Stratus (layer clouds). These are very low-lying, even clouds which float less than 2500 meters/8125 feet above the earth. Stratus cloud cover does not generally have a recognizable structure; it is gray, and brings drizzle.

Cumulus (heap clouds). These are convective clouds formed by warm air currents. They are also known as fair weather clouds. They are at 2000 meters/6500 feet above the ground and seem to constantly unfold, as new cloud rises and then sinks to the side and evaporates.

Nimbostratus (rain layer clouds). These are typical rain clouds which are found at 2000–6000 meters/6500–19,500 feet above the earth. They bring continuous rain if they are thick and large enough.

Altocumulus (middle heap clouds). These clouds, found at 2500–7000 meters/8125–22,750 feet, do not bring rain, but they form great areas of regularly arranged rolls or waves which look like cotton wool.

Altostratus (middle layer cloud). These clouds are a sign that it will rain in the near future. They are blue-gray and the sun shines through them occasionally, but so weakly that it just looks like a pale, faded disc. These clouds are 3000–8000 meters/9750–26,000 feet above the ground.

Cirrocumulus (high fleecy clouds). These are small white clouds which form at a great height (6000–13,000 meters/19,500–42,250 feet), and do not cover the sky. They often appear with cirrostratus clouds, and when this happens they indicate that rain is on the way.

Cirrus (high feathery clouds). Ice clouds which often herald wind or a storm. (6000–13,000 meters/ 19,500–42,250 feet).

Cirrus (feathery clouds)

Cirrocumulus (high fleecy clouds)

Altostratus (middle layer clouds)

Altocumulus (middle heap clouds)

Cumulus (heap clouds)

Nimbostratus (rain layer clouds)

Stratus (layer clouds)

How fast do children grow?

A baby begins to grow very fast from the time it is born. It grows as much in the first month as it will later grow in a whole year. But growing does not mean getting taller and wider. The proportions of various parts of the body in relation to one another alter too. A baby has a comparatively large head because its brain makes up 13 per cent of its body, while in adults the brain only accounts for 2 per cent.

Why are some people big and some people small?

A person's size depends on many things: hereditary genes (the size of parents and relatives, for example) environmental influences, and hormones. The so-called growth hormone is responsible for the rate at which a person grows, but nutrition also plays a very important part. If a person doesn't have enough vitamins in his diet, particularly vit-amins A, B_2 and B_6, he may stop growing and become seriously ill. Liver, milk and spinach are good sources of vitamin A; B_2 is found in yeast products, wholemeal bread and nuts; and B_6 is found in cereals and soya beans. Certain body cells get bigger and spread out, while others divide and multiply and so take up more room. The person gets bigger and heavier – he grows.

The four periods of growth in childhood are:

2–4 years: mainly weight gain.
5–7 years: mainly height gain.
8–10 years: mainly weight gain.
11–15 years: mainly height gain.
12–14-year-old girls grow faster than boys. The boys later overtake them, and when fully grown are on average 10 cm/4 inches taller than girls.

Your height can vary even in a single day: you are at your tallest just after you get up in the morning. By the evening you may have shrunk by as much as 2 cm/^{3}/$_4$ inch or 3 cm/1 inch if you have been walking or standing a lot.

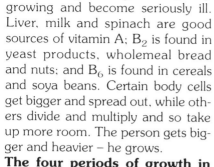

The tallest man in the world was 2.72 meters/8 ft 11 ins high. His name was Robert Wadlow. He died from a badly infected foot when he was 22 years old.

The average height of a European man today is 1.73 meters/5 ft 8 ins.

The smallest man in the world, Calvin Phillips, was only 67 cm/26½ inches high. He didn't live very long, either. He was born in 1791 and died in 1812.

Different nationalities and races not only have different skin colors, but their average height varies as well. The tallest people in the world are the Watussi, who live in Central Africa. The average height of a Watussi man is 1.83 meters/6 feet. The smallest people in the world, the pygmies, also live in Africa, and their menfolk are on average just 1.37 meters/4 ft 6 ins high – about the height of a European ten year-old.

The average rate at which children grow				
Age	Height in cm/ft ins		Weight in kg/lbs ozs	
	Boys	Girls	Boys	Girls
Birth	51/1 8	50/1 7	3.4/7 5	3.3/7 3
3 months	62/2	59/1 11	5.8/12 8	5.6/12 3
1 year	75/2 5	74/2 5	10.3/22 7	9.8/21 6
5 years	110/3 7	109/3 6	18.5/40 8	17.7/39
7 years	122/4	119/3 10	22.5/49 6	22.4/49 4
10 years	137/4 8	135/4 5	30.0/66 15	29.0/64
11 years	140/4 7	140/4 7	32.4/71 5	31.5/69 5
13 years	149/4 10	151/4 11	38.0/83 8	40.0/88 2
15 years	161/5 3	160/5 3	48.0/105 8	49.0/108

In the first six months of its life, a baby grows up to 17 cm/6¾ inches, as much as a child grows in the years between its eighth and twelfth birthdays. By the time he is one year old, he will have grown 24 cm/9½ inches – half as much again as he measured at birth. A baby seems out of proportion when compared with the proportions of an adult's body. His head is enormous and his stomach is big, but his arms and legs are short.

How tall are women?
The average height is 1.65 meters/ 5 ft 5 ins, but any height between 1.48 meters/4 ft 10 ins and 1.75 meters/ 5 ft 5 ins is normal. Other vital statistics:
(Average) Bust: 92 cm/37 inches
Waist: 74 cm/29 inches
Hips: 96.5 cm/38 inches

How tall are men?
(Average) Height: 1.75 meters/5 ft 9 ins
Chest: 98.5 cm/39 inches
Waist: 80.6 cm/31 inches
Hips: 96 cm/38 inches
Normal height band: Between 1.62 meters/5 ft 3 ins and 1.88 meters/6 ft 2 ins

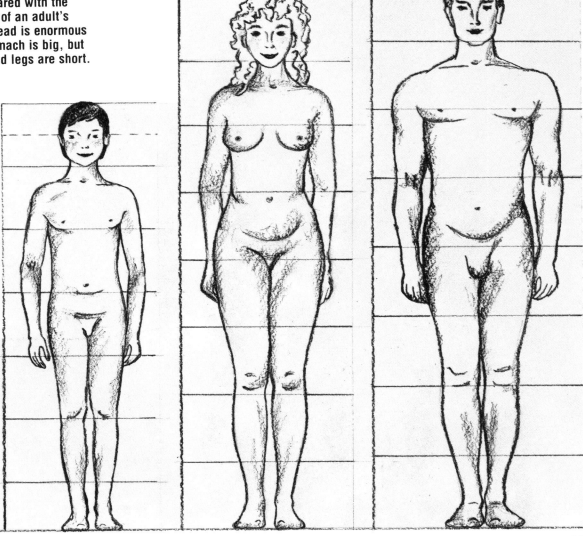

Old people get shorter: from the age of 50, they shrink up to 1 cm/½ inch a year.

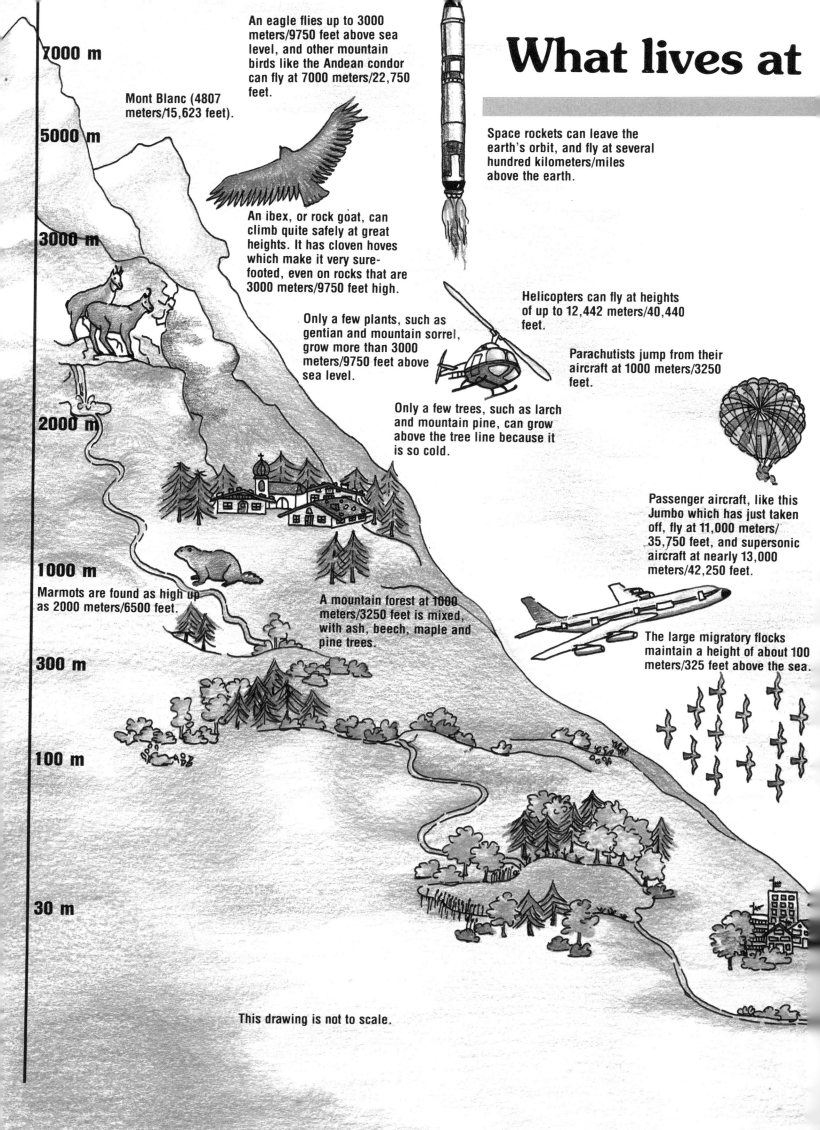

What lives at

7000 m

5000 m

3000 m

2000 m

1000 m

300 m

100 m

30 m

An eagle flies up to 3000 meters/9750 feet above sea level, and other mountain birds like the Andean condor can fly at 7000 meters/22,750 feet.

Mont Blanc (4807 meters/15,623 feet).

An ibex, or rock goat, can climb quite safely at great heights. It has cloven hoves which make it very sure-footed, even on rocks that are 3000 meters/9750 feet high.

Only a few plants, such as gentian and mountain sorrel, grow more than 3000 meters/9750 feet above sea level.

Only a few trees, such as larch and mountain pine, can grow above the tree line because it is so cold.

Marmots are found as high up as 2000 meters/6500 feet.

A mountain forest at 1000 meters/3250 feet is mixed, with ash, beech, maple and pine trees.

This drawing is not to scale.

Space rockets can leave the earth's orbit, and fly at several hundred kilometers/miles above the earth.

Helicopters can fly at heights of up to 12,442 meters/40,440 feet.

Parachutists jump from their aircraft at 1000 meters/3250 feet.

Passenger aircraft, like this Jumbo which has just taken off, fly at 11,000 meters/ 35,750 feet, and supersonic aircraft at nearly 13,000 meters/42,250 feet.

The large migratory flocks maintain a height of about 100 meters/325 feet above the sea.

The higher you climb up a mountain, the colder it gets. The temperature drops ·7°C every 100 meters/325 feet, so it could be 33°C at the foot of Mont Blanc, but only 0°C at the summit. A sharp, icy wind blows high up, the air pressure drops, and there is less oxygen around. This means that the higher people climb, the faster they have to breathe. The same applies to animals. Some animals are particularly well adapted to living at a high altitude. The Tibetan yak lives at heights of more than 6000 meters/19,500 feet, the chamois and the white weasel live at 4000 meters/13,000 feet in the European Alps, and a toad has even been found at 8000 meters/26,000 feet in the Himalayas.

Humans cannot live at heights like these. Only very experienced mountaineers are able to climb mountains without oxygen equipment. Of course, modern technology has meant that people can reach much greater heights in aircraft. But in an airplane, oxygen has to be pumped into the various cabins. A temperature of 20°C is maintained, and the air pressure is equivalent to the pressure of about 2000 meters/6500 feet, although the plane may be flying at 11,000 meters/35,750 feet.

The first people to fly in a hot-air balloon were Jacques-Étienne and Joseph-Michel Montgolfier. In April 1783 the brothers reached a height of 300 meters/975 feet in their balloon. Two hundred years later, the record height for a hot-air balloon is 16,800 meters/54,600 feet. Model remote-controlled airplanes can fly at up to 8200 meters/26,650 feet. Passenger aircraft fly at heights of 11,000–12,000 meters/35,750–39,000

feet and supersonic aircraft at 12,800 meters/41,600 feet. But there are airplanes which can fly three times as high as that, as a Russian pilot proved. He set the world record for the highest flight when he reached an altitude of 37,600 meters/122,200 feet. Satellites are put into orbit about 550 km/344 miles above the earth.

The highest town in the world is Wenchuan (China), at 5100 meters/16,575 feet above sea level. The highest village in Britain is Flash, in North Staffordshire, at 462 meters/1501 feet above sea level. The town of Juf, in the Swiss canton of Graubünden, lies at 2126 meters/6910 feet above sea level, and its inhabitants stay there even during the bitterly cold winters. The highest permanently inhabited dwellings on earth are at 6000 meters/19,500 feet in the Himalayas and in the South American Andes.

These mountaineers were the first to reach the summit:

J. Balmat and M. Pacaw (France) Mont Blanc, 1776

M. Paradis (France), first woman to summit of Mont Blanc, 1808

Edward Whymper (Britain) Matterhorn, 1871

Lucy Walker (Britain), first woman to summit of Matterhorn, 1871

Edmund Hillary (New Zealand) and Tensing Norgay Everest, 1953

Junko Tabei (Japan), first woman to summit of Everest, 1975

These are the heights above sea level of some capital cities:

Vienna	172 m/560 ft
Berne	540 m/1755 ft
Jerusalem	763 m/2480 ft
Johannesburg	1753 m/5700 ft
Cairo	30 m/97 ft
La Paz (Bolivian seat of government)	3600 m/11,700 ft
Lhasa (Tibet; highest capital city in the world)	3650 m/11,865 ft
Mexico City	2240 m/7280 ft
Tokyo	9 m/29 ft
Andorra (highest capital city in Europe)	1061 m/3450 ft

The Montgolfier brothers were able to rise 300 meters/975 feet into the air in the first manned hot-air balloon. You can fly homemade kites at about 160 meters/520 feet high.

Swallows do not fly very high. Their average height is less than 30 meters/98 feet.

How many babies do mammals

Mammals are the most highly developed vertebrate animals and have several things in common. Most of them live on land, breathe with lungs, have hair, suckle their young with milk from mammary glands, and their offspring are born live.

Wild animals have their offspring in the warm seasons of the year when there is plenty of food, so that the young animals can grow as sturdy as possible before the winter. Humans and domestic animals are exceptions to this rule: their babies can be born at any time during the year.

Some people think that big animals have large numbers of young and a long gestation period (this is the time the mother carries the baby animals inside her), and small animals have fewer young and a shorter gestation period, but this is not true. A wild boar, for example, has a very

large litter, but a gestation period of only four months. Another variety of boar, which is roughly the same size, has a litter of only two babies and carries them for five months.

How long before the baby is born?	
Elephant	22 months
Camel	13 months
Donkey	12 months
Horse	11 months
Chimpanzee	9 months
Cow	285 days
Human	265 days
Sheep and goat	roughly 150 days
Pig	115 days
Cat	65 days
Dog	63 days
Hedgehog	50 days
Kangaroo	about 40 days
Rabbit	28–30 days
House mouse and brown rat	21 days
Hamster	20 days

Whales are mammals, despite the fact that they live in water. The blue whale calf is the largest baby mammal of all. At birth it is 6.5–8.6 meters/21–28 feet long, and weighs up to 3000 kg/6600 lb, which is almost as heavy as a fully grown female elephant (3500 kg/7700 lb). An elephant calf, on the other hand, only weighs 121 kg/266 lb, but even this is more than the weight of three twelve-year-old children (35 kg/77 lb each). A baby kangaroo is tiny. It is only 3 cm/1¼ inches long at birth. It immediately finds its way into its mother's pouch and is fed there for eight months. Although kangaroos are bigger and heavier than humans, the gestation period of a kangaro is only 40 days, whereas human pregnancy lasts for more than six times that long (265 days).

Multiple births in humans are not very common. Out of 600,000 babies born in a year, roughly 7500 are twins, there are 90 sets of triplets and one set of quadruplets (four babies). Quintuplets (five babies) and sextuplets (six babies) are very rare. Out of 127 million babies born every year in the whole world, there are only about three sets of quintuplets, and a set of sextuplets is born only once every 25 years.

An elephant mother takes her time – her gestation period lasts nearly two years.

Reproduction

Mares have to be fairly swift about rearing their foals. A mare can be fertilized again just 11 days after giving birth, so a young foal may be suckling from its mother while a new baby is developing inside her. This short fertilization period means that mares are capable of having a foal every year, even though they have an 11-month gestation period. A kangaroo sometimes has three young at the same time: one developing inside her, one in the pouch, and an older one which is running around but still suckles from her.

Hamsters, house mice and brown rats are particularly industrious mothers. A female hamster is able to have a litter of 5–7 babies every 20 days – that's 120 baby hamsters in a year. A house mouse can also have more than 100 babies a year. Her gestation period is 21 days and she has 4–8 baby mice in each litter. The brown rat really is a Supermum. Every 21 days she can give birth to 10–12 baby rats – 190 in a year!

Which mammals have the longest and shortest gestation periods? It takes almost two years before a baby elephant is ready to be born, somewhere between 609–760 days. At the other end of the scale, a type of Australian marten (*Dasyurus viverrinus*) has the shortest gestation period – eight days precisely. The American opossum takes 12–13 days to produce its young.

A word of comfort to anyone who is scared of mice: they only multiply quickly when there are no predators around, and that is rare. Usually only two or three baby mice or rats survive from each litter.

How many young are there in each litter?

Elephant, camel, donkey, Horse, chimpanzee and cow	1
Sheep	1–3
Goat	1–3
Pig	up to 10
Cat	2–6
Dog	2–10
Hedgehog	3–6 (up to 10)
Kangaroo	1
Rabbit	3–10
Hamster	5–7
Brown rat	10–12

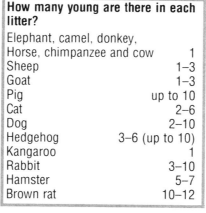

Hamsters are brilliant at having babies! Female hamsters can have 200 babies in the same time as an elephant takes to produce one.

Are birds the only creatures

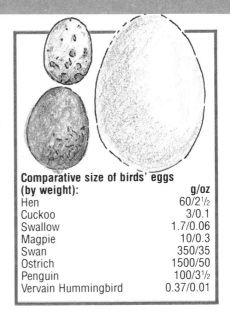

Eggs are female reproductive cells. If the eggs are fertilized by male sperm, a new life is formed within the egg. The eggs of humans and other mammals develop inside the mother's body. The unborn baby receives the nutrients it needs directly from the mother and is also extremely well protected. The eggs of birds, reptiles and insects develop outside the mother's body. Birds and reptiles lay eggs with a tough protective covering or shell. So do sharks, common snails and certain insects. Other fish, as well as amphibians and molluscs, lay soft eggs called spawn, which are surrounded by a jelly-like substance.

Comparative size of birds' eggs (by weight):	g/oz
Hen	60/2½
Cuckoo	3/0.1
Swallow	1.7/0.06
Magpie	10/0.3
Swan	350/35
Ostrich	1500/50
Penguin	100/3½
Vervain Hummingbird	0.37/0.01

Why do bird's eggs have so many different colors and patterns? The egg cells of a bird are formed in its ovary. First, the egg cell or ovum is surrounded by egg yolk. Albumen then forms in the upper section of the oviduct around this nucleus. It is surrounded by a very thin, parchment-like membrane. Lastly, the shell, which contains calcium, begins to form further down the oviduct. It starts off almost transparent, but as it makes its way to the outside it presses against glands which contain coloring matter. The patterns on the shell are caused by the direction and varying speeds of the egg's movements as it twists and turns through the oviduct. A bird produces, on average, one egg per day. The tiny fledgling inside the egg does not begin to develop until the egg has been laid in the nest. The egg is incubated, or kept warm, by the parent bird as the fledgling grows and finally hatches out.

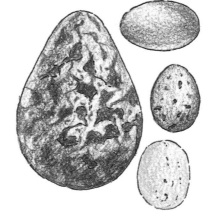

Birds' eggs vary in size and their patterns are never the same.

Some animals do not look after their eggs as birds do. These animals have to lay a great many eggs to make sure that at least some will hatch before they are destroyed or eaten by other creatures. The carp spawns more than half a million eggs per year and just swims away from them. The stickleback lays only about 100 eggs per year, but it takes very good care of its offspring.

An egg is made up of at least 80 per cent water, 13 per cent nitrogenous substance, and about 7 per cent minerals. It is not only a protective covering for the living creature inside it, but is also the creature's source of nutrition. It is a perfect store cupboard of everything that the baby creature needs: protein, lecithin, cholesterol, fatty oil and salts.

Did you know that a hen's egg, whether boiled, fried or poached, is as nourishing as 50 g/2 oz beef?

Penguins incubate their eggs standing up, to protect the eggs from the cold. The baby penguin emerges from its shell after 63 days.

Turtles lay many eggs. The leatherback, or leathery turtle, lays up to 1000, which she buries in the hot tropical sand to be incubated by the heat of the sun. When they have hatched, the baby turtles have to burrow up through the sand before they see daylight for the first time.

Insects lay eggs, too. In their case, however, it is not small insects which hatch out of the eggs, but larvae or grubs, which later pupate, or turn into pupae. Only after this stage, also known as the metamorphosis, do the young insects emerge.

How long do the different stages of development take?

	Size of egg	No. of eggs	Egg development	Larva	Pupa
Housefly	1 mm/ 0.04 inch	about 200 several times a year	12–24 hours, sometimes 4 days	6–7 days	8 days
Clothes moth	Smaller than 1 mm/ 0.04 inch	up to 220	depends on temperature: 12 days (at 20°C) 7 days (at 20–25°C)	several months	14–44 days
Honey bee	1.3–1.5 mm/0.05–0.06 inch	1.5 million in a lifetime	3 days	depends on whether worker bee, drone or queen: between 7–12 days	between 5 and 15 days

How many eggs do hens lay? A domestic hen lays more than 200 eggs a year, each of them weighing 60 g/2½ oz. When the hen is broody, she lays 12–18 eggs in her nest day after day. She sits on the eggs for 20–22 days until the baby chicks hatch out. In comparison with this:

Birds	Number of eggs	Incubation period (days)
Duck	10–15	26–30
Goose	12–15	28–32
Cuckoo	10–15	11–13 (by foster parents)
Song thrush	5–6	12–14
Sparrow	5–6	13–14
Swallow	4–5	14–16
Magpie	6–8	17–18
Ostrich	30	40
Emperor penguin	1	63
Reptiles		
Grass snake	15–35	63
Mud turtle	9–11	48
Leatherback (leathery turtle)	up to 1000	more than 100
Alligator	30–60	61
Crocodile	90–100	40–60

Why do bad eggs smell so awful? When an egg goes bad, hydrogen sulphide gas is produced inside it, and this gives it its dreadful smell. You can tell how fresh an egg is by putting it into water. If it's fresh, it will sink straight to the bottom. A week-old egg will not quite sit on the bottom, and old eggs float.

Frogs' eggs are tiny, and are called frogspawn. Like the eggs of nearly all fish, amphibians and molluscs, the frogs' eggs are soft and are surrounded by a jelly-like substance. They are laid in strings or clumps in the water and are fertilized by the male. The tadpoles develop from the frogspawn, and later turn into frogs.

The fruit fly is the fastest fly of all to develop. It takes less than a day for a fruit fly larva to form from the egg. This larva then eats for 7 days, after which it pupates. Five days later the young fruit fly emerges from the pupa.

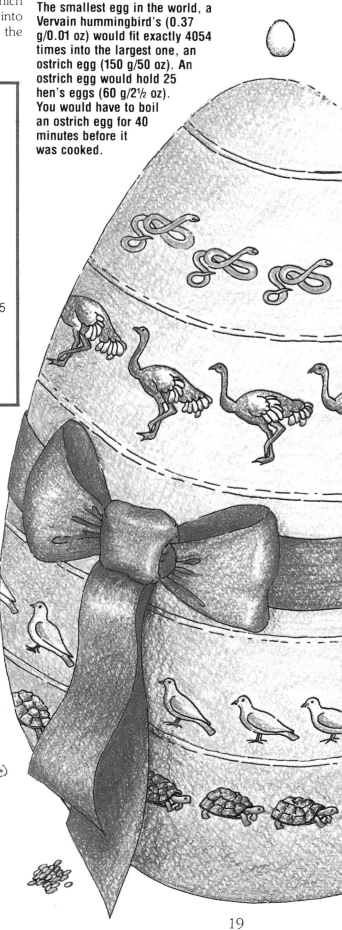

The smallest egg in the world, a Vervain hummingbird's (0.37 g/0.01 oz) would fit exactly 4054 times into the largest one, an ostrich egg (150 g/50 oz). An ostrich egg would hold 25 hen's eggs (60 g/2½ oz). You would have to boil an ostrich egg for 40 minutes before it was cooked.

How quickly do mammals

Human babies cannot stand or walk, or move themselves along at all for some months after they are born. Some other mammals have babies which can stand and walk, and even eat, as soon as they are born. Mammals grow at different rates, and some mature much more quickly than others. Humans take the longest of all to develop from a baby into an adult – 18-20 years.

How long does it take for mammals to become mature adults?
The smaller mammals grow much faster than larger ones, which is why they mature more quickly and are able to have their own young much earlier. The following list shows the growth rate of some mammals:

House mouse	5–6 weeks
Golden hamster	4–6 weeks
Water rat	2 months
Squirrel	3–4 months
Rabbit	5–8 months
Hare	6–8 months
Beaver	1 year
Hedgehog	1 year
Deer	1½ years
Panda	2–3 years
Wolf	3 years
Otter	3 years
Chamois	3 years
Bear	4 years
Camel	4 years
Hippopotamus	5–6 years
Elephant	12–15 years
Long-tailed monkey	3 years
Chimpanzee	8–10 years

How big are mammals and how big are their babies?

	Mother's weight	No. in litter	Weight of litter	Weight of one baby
Field mouse	31 g/1 oz	8	15.6 g/0.5 oz	1.95/0.06 oz
Guinea pig	700 g/25 oz	4	320 g/11½ oz	80 g/3 oz
House mouse	25 g/1 oz	8	10 g/0.3 oz	1.25 g/0.04 oz
Rat	138 g/5 oz	6	52 g/2 oz	8.6 g/0.3 oz
Rabbit	1175 g/42 oz	5	233 g/8 oz	46.6 g/2 oz
Fox	4200 g/150 oz	7	680 g/24 oz	97.1 g/3 oz
Cat	2750 g/98 oz	4	452 g/16 oz	113 g/4 oz
Hedgehog	725 g/26 oz	7	98 g/3½ oz	14 g/0.5 oz
Goat	62 kg/137 lb	2	6.4 kg/14 lb	3.2 kg/7 lb
Horse	800 kg/1777 lb	1	71 kg/157 lb	71 kg/157 lb
Gorilla	60 kg/133 lb	1	3.2 kg/7 lb	3.2 kg/7 lb
Chimpanzee	46 kg/ 102 lb	1	1.8 kg/4 lb	1.8 kg/4 lb
Lion	114 kg/253 lb	5	4.4 kg/11 lb	0.88 kg/2 lb
Elephant	3000 kg/6666 lb	1	93 kg/206 lb	93 kg/206 lb
Hippopotamus	1750 kg/3888 lb	1	40 kg/88 lb	40 kg/88 lb
Blue whale	79,000 kg/175,555 lb	1	2000 kg/4444 lb	2000 kg/4444 lb
Brown bear	250 kg/555 lb	1	0.5 kg/1 lb	0.5 kg/1 lb
Panda	113 kg/251 lb	1	0.141 kg/5 oz	0.141 kg/0.3 lb

It is 8–10 years before a chimpanzee reaches adulthood.

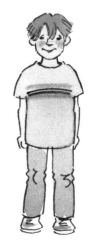

Humans take 18–20 years.

A mouse is a fully grown adult at 5–6 weeks.

Bear cubs are fully grown bears in 4 years.

A red deer is fully grown and mature at 18 months.

Mammals

Panda bear cubs are tiny, blind and toothless at birth. They weigh around 140 g/5 oz, and their mothers are about 800 times their size. The cubs grow very quickly. At 8 weeks they are already 20 times heavier than they were at birth. (A human takes 18 years to reach this level). A panda is sexually mature and therefore an adult after 2–3 years. Pandas seldom live longer than 14 years.

How fast can mammals move?

Most mammals can move very much faster than an 11-year-old child. Compare these speeds:

Man (walking pace)	5 kph/3.1 mph
11-year-old child (running)	10 kph/6.2 mph
Greenland whale	7.2 kph/4.5 mph
Horse (walking)	7.2 kph/4.5 mph
House rat	9.5 kph/6 mph
House mouse	12 kph/7.5 mph
Horse (trotting)	13.5 kph/8.4 mph
Indian elephant	23.4 kph/14.6 mph
Man (running)	28.8–36 kph/ 18–22.5 mph
Horse (galloping)	36 kph/22.5 mph
Rabbit	38 kph/23.7 mph
Polar bear	40 kph/25 mph
Man (in 100 meter sprint)	44.88 kph/28 mph
Giraffe	48 kph/30 mph
Gray kangaroo	64 kph/40 mph
African elephant	67 kph/41.9 mph
Common hare	72 kph/45 mph
Lion	75 kph/46.9 mph
Grayhound	110 kph/68.7 mph
Cheetah	96.6–120 kph/60–75 mph

How much milk do domestic animals produce per year?

European cow:
4000–5000 liters/
8500–10,600 pints

Indian cow:
200–300 liters/
425–640 pints

Goat:
60–800 liters/
1280–1700 pints

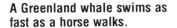

A cow produces five times more milk in a year than a goat.

How much milk do domestic animals produce per day?

European cow:
11–14 liters/
23–30 pints.

Indian cow:
0.55–0.8 liters/
1.2–1.7 pints

Goat:
1.6–2.2 liters/
3.4–4.7 pints.

A Greenland whale swims as fast as a horse walks.

How deep can deep-sea divers

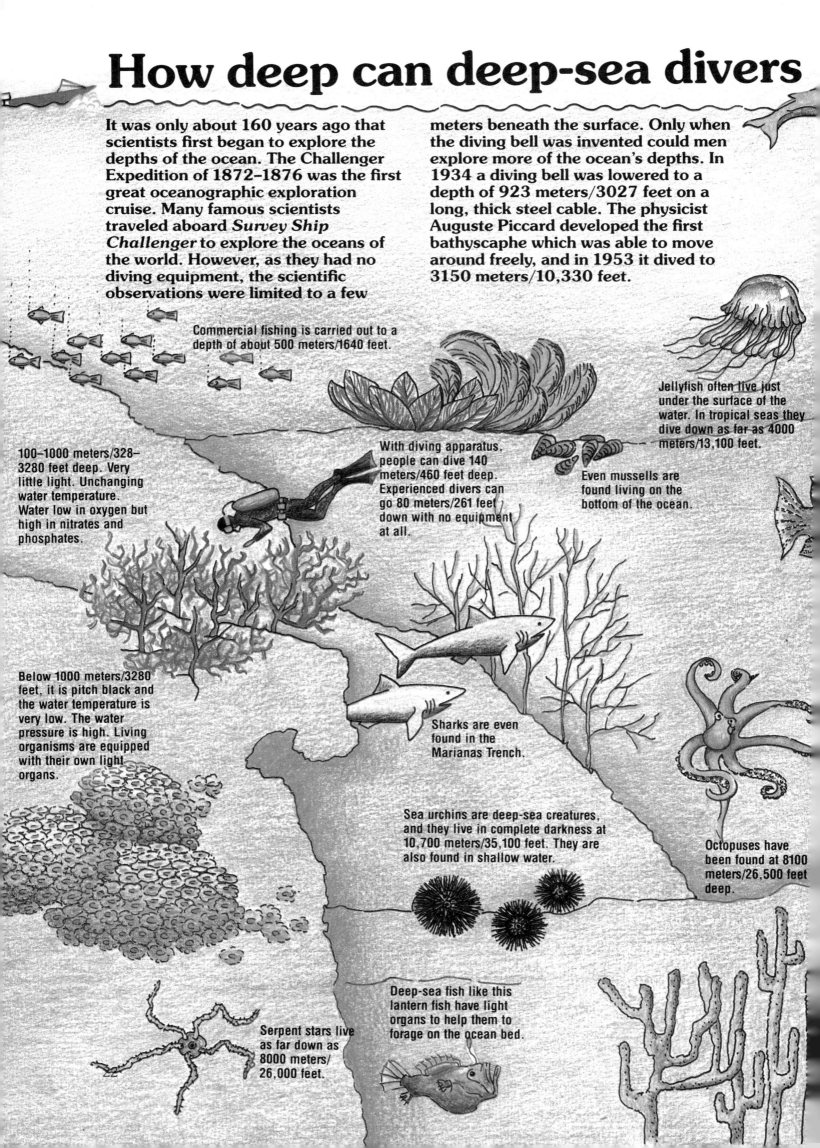

It was only about 160 years ago that scientists first began to explore the depths of the ocean. The Challenger Expedition of 1872–1876 was the first great oceanographic exploration cruise. Many famous scientists traveled aboard *Survey Ship Challenger* to explore the oceans of the world. However, as they had no diving equipment, the scientific observations were limited to a few meters beneath the surface. Only when the diving bell was invented could men explore more of the ocean's depths. In 1934 a diving bell was lowered to a depth of 923 meters/3027 feet on a long, thick steel cable. The physicist Auguste Piccard developed the first bathyscaphe which was able to move around freely, and in 1953 it dived to 3150 meters/10,330 feet.

Commercial fishing is carried out to a depth of about 500 meters/1640 feet.

Jellyfish often live just under the surface of the water. In tropical seas they dive down as far as 4000 meters/13,100 feet.

100–1000 meters/328–3280 feet deep. Very little light. Unchanging water temperature. Water low in oxygen but high in nitrates and phosphates.

With diving apparatus, people can dive 140 meters/460 feet deep. Experienced divers can go 80 meters/261 feet down with no equipment at all.

Even mussels are found living on the bottom of the ocean.

Below 1000 meters/3280 feet, it is pitch black and the water temperature is very low. The water pressure is high. Living organisms are equipped with their own light organs.

Sharks are even found in the Marianas Trench.

Sea urchins are deep-sea creatures, and they live in complete darkness at 10,700 meters/35,100 feet. They are also found in shallow water.

Octopuses have been found at 8100 meters/26,500 feet deep.

Deep-sea fish like this lantern fish have light organs to help them to forage on the ocean bed.

Serpent stars live as far down as 8000 meters/26,000 feet.

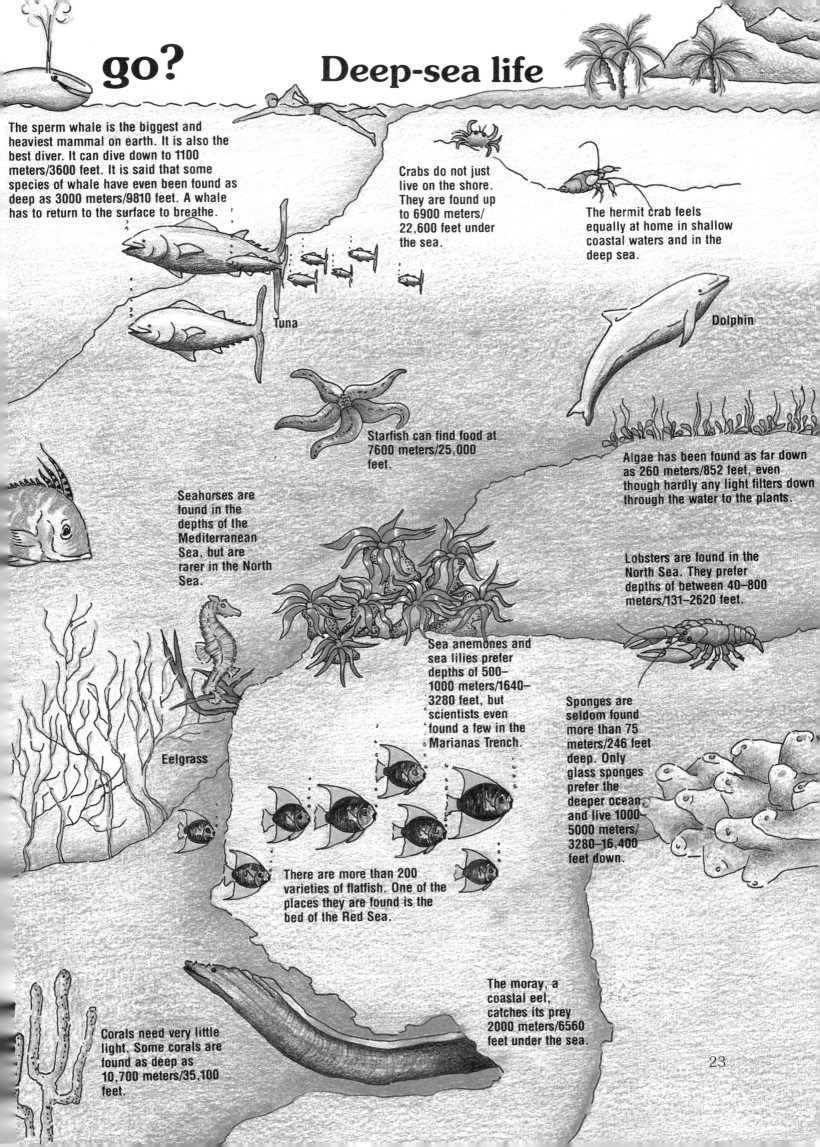

go?

Deep-sea life

The sperm whale is the biggest and heaviest mammal on earth. It is also the best diver. It can dive down to 1100 meters/3600 feet. It is said that some species of whale have even been found as deep as 3000 meters/9810 feet. A whale has to return to the surface to breathe.

Crabs do not just live on the shore. They are found up to 6900 meters/ 22,600 feet under the sea.

The hermit crab feels equally at home in shallow coastal waters and in the deep sea.

Tuna

Dolphin

Starfish can find food at 7600 meters/25,000 feet.

Algae has been found as far down as 260 meters/852 feet, even though hardly any light filters down through the water to the plants.

Seahorses are found in the depths of the Mediterranean Sea, but are rarer in the North Sea.

Lobsters are found in the North Sea. They prefer depths of between 40–800 meters/131–2620 feet.

Sea anemones and sea lilies prefer depths of 500–1000 meters/1640–3280 feet, but scientists even found a few in the Marianas Trench.

Eelgrass

Sponges are seldom found more than 75 meters/246 feet deep. Only glass sponges prefer the deeper ocean, and live 1000–5000 meters/3280–16,400 feet down.

There are more than 200 varieties of flatfish. One of the places they are found is the bed of the Red Sea.

The moray, a coastal eel, catches its prey 2000 meters/6560 feet under the sea.

Corals need very little light. Some corals are found as deep as 10,700 meters/35,100 feet.

23

Who lives the longest?

All living creatures have three characteristics in common. Firstly they have to have food, and they have to breathe. Secondly, they have instinctive reactions, so if they are hungry, they look for food; if they are cold, they seek warmth; if they are tired, they sleep. And finally, they continue to develop throughout their lives: they grow, learn, and have offspring to ensure that their species does not die out. Anything without these three characteristics is not a living being.

Yet every creature has its own special requirements, too: Some live in water, others live on land. Certain life forms need to be kept cold whilst others need to be warm. And one creature's food varies enormously from another's. Some creatures eat plants and others eat animals. Some creatures eat both. Certain creatures such as the mayfly, live for only a few hours, and others live for many years.

How long do they live?

There is a difference between the average life expectancy of a creature or plant, and the longest it ever lives, which only happens when conditions are particularly favorable. Trees are not creatures, of course, but they are alive and they have a lifespan. They can live longer than any other living things. Certain trees have a maximum lifespan of more than 1000 years, some live even longer than that.

Maximum lifespan of some trees:

Baobab: 5000 years
Bristlecone pine: 4600 years
Sequoia (redwood): 4000 years
Pedunculate oak: 1500 years
Lime: 800–1000 years
Beech: 600–1000 years
Elm: 500 years
Conifers: 300–500 years
Black poplar: 150 years
Blueberry (bush): 25 years

What is the longest an animal can live?

Animal	Lifespan	Animal	Lifespan
Elephant	80 years	Cat	36 years
Chimpanzee, orang-utan		Vulture	100 years
and gorilla	60 years	Goose	49 years
Horse	61 years	Eagle	30 years
Donkey	100 years	Stork	70 years
Cow	30 years	Owl	70 years
Sheep	28 years	Pigeon	53 years
Goat	20 years	Seagull	55 years
Hippopotamus	40 years	Blackbird	18 years
Rhinoceros	45 years	Starling	14 years
Wolf	15 years	Canary	34 years
Fox	10 years	Mallard	20 years
Lion	40 years	Sturgeon	150 years
Brown bear	50 years	Pike	70 years
Beaver	50 years	Carp	50 years
Guinea pig	14 years	Plaice	80 years
Rabbit	18 years	Herring	15 years
House mouse	7 years	Mud turtle	120 years
Dog	29 years	Tortoise	150 years
Alligator	66 years		

People used not to live as long as they do today. Thanks to modern advances in medicine and better health care, people live nearly twice as long as they did 100 years ago.

Average life expectancy (in years)		
	Men	**Women**
2000 years ago	33	27
100 years ago	35	38
80 years ago	45	48
20 years ago	68	74
Today	70	77

People in industrial societies live longer than inhabitants of the poorer countries of the world.

Around the world (average lifespan in years)		
	Men	**Women**
Japan	74	80
Great Britain	67	73
USA	68	76
Switzerland	72	79
Austria	69	77
Germany	70	74

In poorer countries, people do not live so long

Gabon (Africa)	35 years
Upper Volta (Africa)	41 years
Sudan (Africa)	43 years
Ethiopia (Africa)	45 years
Bolivia (South America)	46 years
Nigeria (Africa)	50 years
India	55 years

Tortoises live much longer than people. If you look at the facts on these pages, you can see that man has a long lifespan – compared with many creatures. But tortoises live more than twice as long as people do – up to 150 years, in fact. Imagine, if your grandmother had got a baby tortoise for her sixth birthday and if she had looked after it well, that tortoise would still have been alive when your grandmother had grandchildren and great-grandchildren, even when her great, great, great-grandchild was born! But the saying that tortoises grow to be as old as Methuselah is too far-fetched. The ancient biblical Methuselah is supposed to have lived 969 years! (Fantastic, even though a year in those days was much shorter than it is now!)

Where does water boil at 71°C?

Not all thermometers are the same. Some measure in degrees Celsius (or Centigrade), some in degrees Fahrenheit. For scientific purposes, a third scale is often used. This is the Kelvin scale, which begins at absolute zero, the temperature at which thermal energy vanishes and it can get no colder. It corresponds to −273.16° on the Celsius scale. The Fahrenheit scale is named after the German physicist, Gabriel Fahrenheit, who invented the mercury thermometer and devised the scale for it. On this scale, the melting point of ice is 32°F, normal blood temperature is 100°F, and the boiling point of water is 212°F. Another scale, the Rankine scale, is used in industry. A fifth one, the Reaumur scale, is no longer used.

Temperature Scales		
K	°C	°F
373.16	100	212
363.16	90	194
353.16	80	176
343.16	70	158
333.16	60	140
323.16	50	122
313.16	40	104
310.93	37.78	100
310	37	98.6
303.16	30	86
293.16	20	68
283.16	10	50
273.16	0	32
263.16	−10	14
255.37	−17.78	0
253.16	−20	−4
243.16	−30	−22
23.16	−40	−40
200	−73.16	−99.67
100	−173.16	−279.67
0	−273.16	−459.67

This table shows the corresponding temperatures on the different scales.

Water boils at different temperatures at different places on the earth. The higher up you live, the lower the temperature at which water boils, and vice versa. This is because the atmospheric pressure decreases at higher altitudes (atmospheric pressure is the weight of the air pressing down on the earth). The lower the pressure, the lower the boiling point of water. And the opposite is also true. The pressure is greater in low-lying regions and so more heat is needed to boil water.

In London and Hamburg, which both lie roughly at sea level, water boils at 10°C. In the Dead Sea area, which lies 396 meters/1300 feet below sea level, it boils at 101°C. In Denver (USA), Johannesburg (South Africa) and Davos (Switzerland), which lie at 1600–1700 meters/5250–5575 feet above sea level, water boils at 95°C. In Quito (Ecuador), 2850 meters/9400 feet above sea level, it boils at 90°C, while in Lhasa (Tibet) and La Paz (Bolivia), cities which are both more than 3600 meters/11,800 feet above sea level, it boils at 87°C. On the summit of Mount Everest, which is 8848 meters/29,000 feet high, water will boil at 71°C.

In lands which lie more or less at sea level, water boils at 100°C. In Lhasa (capital of Tibet), it boils at 87°C. The rice which is the staple diet of Tibet has to be cooked for much longer before it is done!

There is an enormous variation between the highest and the lowest temperatures recorded.

Temperatures (in °C)

Absolute zero	−273.16
Lowest artificially produced temperature	−273.149985
Moon (dark side)	−162
Coldest air temperature (Antarctica)	−89.2
Air 20 km/12.5 miles above the earth	−60
Freezing point of sea water	−2.5
Freezing point of fresh water	0
Temperature of melting ice	0
Ocean floor (average)	4
Human body temperature	37
Feverish temperature (human)	up to 42
1000 meters/3280 feet below earth's surface	50
Warmest air temperature (Aziziyah, Libya)	58
Boiling point of water	100
Moon (bright side)	117
Charcoal fire	800
Brown coal/lignite fire	1100
Blacksmith's fire	1250
Pottery kiln	1300
Iron foundry	1350
Hard coal/mineral coal fire	1400
Element in electric light bulb	2300
Center of the earth	4000–12,000
Surface of the sun	5700
Highest artificially produced temperature	50,000
Center of the sun (corona)	1,000,000
Core of an atomic bomb explosion	20,000,000
Core of a hydrogen bomb explosion	50,000,000

Heat records		Cold records	
Aziziyah (Libya) (highest shade temperature)	58.0°C	Antarctica (lowest temperature)	−89.2°C
Dallol (Ethiopia) (highest mean temperature on earth)	34.4°C	Antarctica (lowest mean temperature on earth)	−58.0°C
Seville (Spain) (highest European temperature)	50.0°C	Sodankylä (Finland) (lowest European temperature)	−45.0°C
Death Valley (USA) (highest temperature in North America)	56.7°C	Floeberg Bay (Canada) (lowest temperature in North America)	−58.3°C

This girl is ill in bed with a temperature of 100° — Fahrenheit, of course. That is 38° Celsius or centigrade.

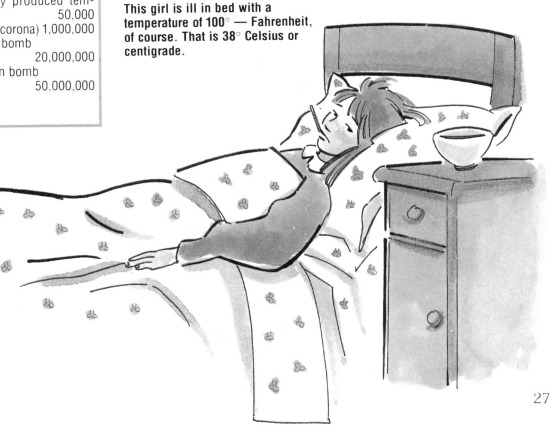

Who can jump the furthest?

An athlete who wants to be a high jump or long jump champion has to have well-developed muscles, particularly in the legs. The muscles are the 'power machines' of the body. Nerve impulses cause the muscles to contract suddenly, making them shorter and thicker, and then to relax again during the jump. This releases the energy for the jumps.

You can see that some animals are built for jumping just by looking at their strong legs. Frogs and kangaroos are two examples. A female sharp-nosed frog set the world record for a triple jump with a jump of 10.3 meters/33.78 feet. A bullfrog, on the other hand, has difficulty in jumping 2 meters/6.56 feet. The longest jump measured for an Australian red kangaroo is 12.8 meters/537 feet. In comparison, the long jump record for a man is 8.9 meters/29.1 feet, held by American Bob Beaman since 1968. Kangaroos beat man at the high jump too. They can jump 3.5 meters/11.48 feet high in one bound. The Swede Jan Sjöberg broke the men's world record in 1987 with 2.42 meters/7.94 feet.

If sportsmen use a long pole to help them, they can jump over much higher obstacles. Up until 1942 bamboo poles were used in pole vaulting, and the world record then was 4.77 meters/15.65 feet. Glass fiber poles, introduced in 1961, are still in use today, and in 1988 Sergei Bubka (USSR) cleared 6.06 meters/19.88 feet.

Showjumping events show how high and how far horses can jump with a rider. The widest jump cleared by a horse over water was 8.40 meters/27.5 feet.

Can fish fly? There is a very distinctive type of fish known as the flying fish. Several species belong to this family. They all appear to fly above the water, like birds through the air. In fact, they jump and glide rather than fly. They build up speed under-water, then use their tail fins to thrust themselves out of the water, while their pectoral fins act as 'wings'. Flying fish can jump 2 meters/6.56 feet.

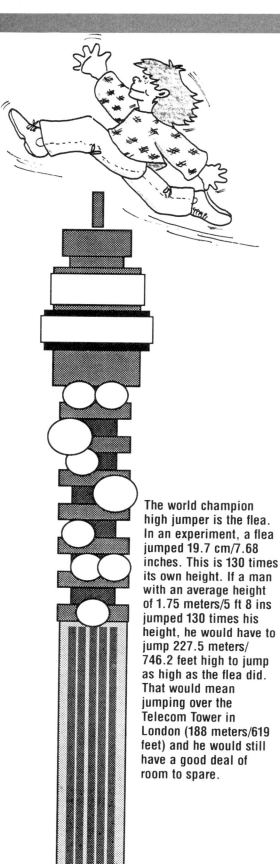

The world champion high jumper is the flea. In an experiment, a flea jumped 19.7 cm/7.68 inches. This is 130 times its own height. If a man with an average height of 1.75 meters/5 ft 8 ins jumped 130 times his height, he would have to jump 227.5 meters/746.2 feet high to jump as high as the flea did. That would mean jumping over the Telecom Tower in London (188 meters/619 feet) and he would still have a good deal of room to spare.

Human jumps					
High jump		Year	**Long jump**		Year
(m/ft)	Men		(m/ft)	Men	
1.70/5.57	F. H. Gooch (GB)	1864	7.61/24.96	P. O'Connor (Ireland)	1901
2/6.56	G. Horine (USA)	1912	7.69/25.22	E. Gourdin (USA)	1921
2.30/7.54	D. Stones (USA)	1976	8.13/26.66	J. Owens (USA)	1935
2.39/18.73	Zhu Jianhua (China)	1984	8.35/27.38	I. Ter-Ovanesyan (USSR)	1967
2.42/7.94	J. Sjöberg (Sweden)	1987	8.90/29.19	R. Beamon (USA)	1968
	Women			Women	
1.65/5.41	J. Shiley (USA)	1932	5.98/19.61	K. Hitomi (Japan)	1928
1.83/6.00	J. Balas (Rumania)	1958	6.12/20.07	C. Schulz (Germany)	1939
1.96/6.42	R. Ackermann (E. Germany)	1976	6.84/22.43	H. Rosendahl (W. Germany)	1970
2.07/6.78	L. Andonova (Bulgaria)	1984	7.43/24.37	A. Cusmir (Rumania)	1983
2.09/6.85	S. Kostadinova (Bulgaria)	1987	7.52/24.66	G. Chistyakova (USSR)	1988

Jumping

Higher and higher, further and further. In 1864, F. H. Gooch (England) set a high jump record of 1.70 meters/5.57 feet. In 1987, Jan Sjöberg (Sweden) jumped 72 cm/2.37 inches higher than that, and set a new men's world record of 2.42 meters/7.94 feet. The women's record is held by S. Kostadinova (Bulgaria) with 2.09 meters/6.85 feet. Between 1912 and 1987, the men's world record improved by 41 cm/15.9 inches (from 2.01–2.42 meters/6.59–7.94 feet). In the same period, the women improved their record by 44 cm/17.16 inches (from 1.65–2.09 meters/5.41–6.85 feet).

Long jump: In 1901, P. O'Connor (Ireland) jumped 7.61 meters/24.96 feet, and in 1968 R. Beamon (USA) cleared 8.90 meters/29.19 feet – 1.21 meters/3.96 feet further. In 1988, Galina Chistyakova (USSR) jumped 7.52 meters/24.66 feet – 1.54 meters/5.05 feet further than K. Hitomi (Japan) in 1928, who jumped 5.98 meters/19.61 feet.

We know that there were jumping events in Roman times. Roman reports show, for example, that the Germanic peoples used to swing themselves on to their horses using poles. They also had an event known as the 'king's jump', which was a cross between a long jump and high jump, and involved leaping over six horses standing side by side.

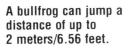

A bullfrog can jump a distance of up to 2 meters/6.56 feet.

A horse can jump 2.5 meters/8.2 feet high, and over a river or water jump 8.5 meters/27.8 feet wide.

A frog can jump several meters/feet to catch prey such as grasshoppers. The grasshopper can jump up to 2 meters/6.56 feet to get away. A jumping mouse has to jump twice to cover the same distance that a tiger covers in one bound – the mouse manages only 2.5 meters/8.2 feet to the tiger's 5 meters/16.4 feet.

People do not jump a great deal, except to break sporting records. There are high jump, pole vaulting, long jump and triple jump events. Skiers jump ski-jumps, and water-skiers jump ramps. Gymnasts have special jumping techniques for apparatus and floor work. Trampolines are used for some types of jumping. Divers use springboards or diving towers to perform their magnificent dives.

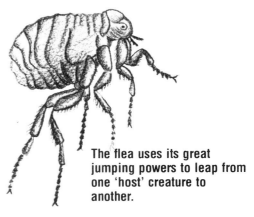

Even when carrying a baby in her pouch, a kangaroo can jump a distance of several meters/feet.

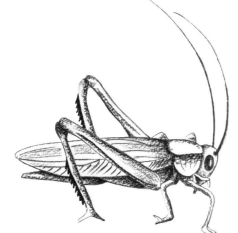

A grasshopper can jump as far as a bullfrog.

Animal jumps (in m/ft)		
Species	Height	Distance
Flea	0.197/0.646	0.33/1.08
Sharp-nosed frog		10.3/33.78
Bullfrog		2/6.56
Grasshopper		2/6.56
Flying fish		2/6.56
Jumping mouse	0.5/1.64	2.5/8.2
Tiger		5.0/16.4
German shepherd dog	3.55/11.64	5.3/17.38
Horse	2.47/8.10	8.4/27.55
Kangaroo	3.2/10.49	12.8/41.99
Hare	2.1/6.88	7/22.96
Puma	2.7/8.86	11/36.08

The flea uses its great jumping powers to leap from one 'host' creature to another.

A German shepherd dog can jump up to 3.55 meters/11.65 feet high. The men's world high jump record is 2.42 meters/7.94 feet.

Where are icebergs found?

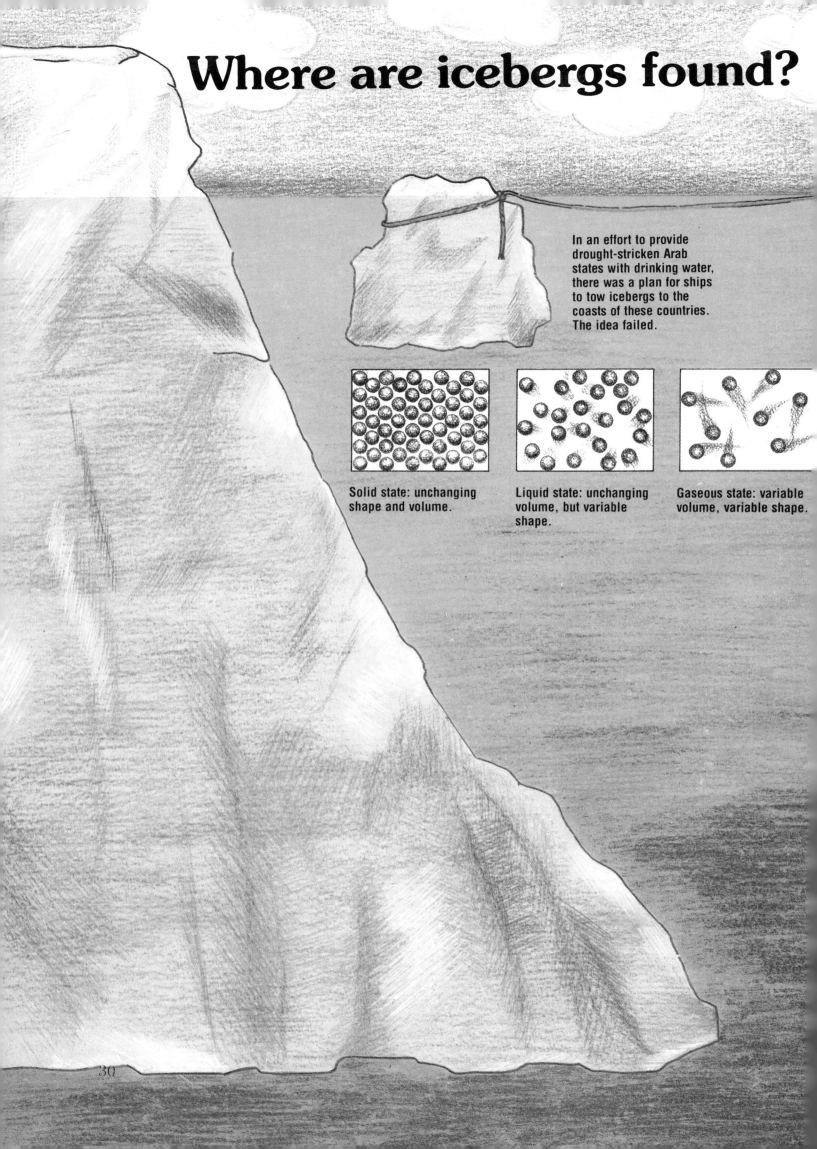

In an effort to provide drought-stricken Arab states with drinking water, there was a plan for ships to tow icebergs to the coasts of these countries. The idea failed.

Solid state: unchanging shape and volume.

Liquid state: unchanging volume, but variable shape.

Gaseous state: variable volume, variable shape.

30

Temperature

Floating icebergs come originally from the ice-cold polar regions. It is so cold there that even the sea freezes and thick ice-floes lie on the surface of the water. Over thousands of years, rain and snow falling on these cause immense icebergs to build up. More than a tenth of the earth's surface is covered with these icy monsters. If they ever melted, the level of the oceans would rise, and many coastal lands would disappear underwater. The frozen surface beneath the iceberg is not stable. The immense weight pressing down on it causes bits to break away and push against other ice-floes. Smaller sections are constantly breaking off at the edges of the huge mass of ice, and these float away as icebergs. But why is water sometimes solid (ice), sometimes liquid and sometimes a gas (steam)?

At temperatures below 0° Celsius, water freezes and becomes ice, and at 100° Celsius it boils and turns into steam. The stability of water is therefore linked to the temperature: when it is very cold, water is solid, and when it is very hot, it turns into a gas. These three forms of water, solid, liquid, and gaseous, are known as its *states*. Every substance has these three states.

In the solid state, a substance remains the same size and shape. This is because the smallest particles of the substance, the atoms, lie still and closely packed together. If the solid state is heated, the atoms start to move about, and the substance becomes liquid and spreads outwards.

If this liquid is heated still further, the atoms move about more rapidly and want to escape from the liquid. The liquid evaporates and turns to gas. The threshold between the solid state and the liquid is known as the melting point, and that between the liquid and the gaseous states is known as the boiling point. Every substance has its own melting and boiling points. That is why there are solids, liquids and gases on earth.

The table shows the temperatures at which a solid substance becomes a liquid (melting point) and a gas (boiling point).

When does a substance turn into a liquid or a gas?

Substance	Melting point (in °C)	Boiling point (in °C)
Aluminum	660.4°	2467°
Lead	327.5°	1740°
Iron	1535°	2750°
Gold	1064.4°	2807°
Copper	1083°	2567°
Neon	−248.7°	−246°
Platinum	1772°	3827°
Mercury	−38.9°	356.6°
Oxygen	−218.4°	−183°
Silver	961.3°	2212°
Uranium	1132°	3818°
Hydrogen	−259.1°	−252.9°
Chloroform	−63.7	61.1°
Carbon dioxide	−56°	−78.5°
Air	−213°	−193°
Water	0°	100°

Thermometer

The Celsius scale is based on the boiling point (100°) and the melting point of (0°) of water. The Kelvin scale is based on another internationally recognized temperature system. It is named after the Englishman, Lord Kelvin of Largs (1824–1907), who did a lot of research into absolute zero, the temperature which is so cold that it cannot get any colder. Absolute zero is 0°K on the Kelvin scale, and −273.16° on the Celsius scale. To convert a temperature in degrees Celsius to one in degrees Kelvin, you add 273.16 to the Celsius temperature.

100 °C
373,16 °K

40 °C
313,16 °K

The fruit of a plant is the storehouse for its seeds. Plants are fertilized by pollen, which is carried by bees or the wind from a male plant to the ovules (eggs) in the flower or ovary of a female plant. The fertilized ovules develop into seeds and the ovary itself forms a fruit. This consists of an outer layer called the pericarp, which nourishes and protects the seeds inside.

The vitamins found in edible fruit are vital for human nutrition. Each fruit belongs to a particular group, depending on how it is made up: there are stone fruits or drupes (cherries, plums); pseudocarps, or false fruits (apples, strawberries, pineapples); multiple fruits (blackberries); berry fruits (gooseberries); pulses (peas, beans); nuts (hazelnuts), and others.

The plant has to spread its seeds so that they can grow. They have different ways of doing this. Maples and sycamore have 'winged' fruit which spin through the air and are often carried far away from the parent tree by the wind. Oak and beech trees have cup fruits, which sit in cup-like holders. Touch-me-not is a plant with seed pods that burst open at a touch when ripe, scattering the seeds. Hazelnuts are 'closed' fruits, which have only one seed in a hard tightly closed shell. Pines have cones which contain seeds. The cones are cracked open by birds and animals and the seeds are spread.

You cannot always tell straight away what family certain fruits belong to. For example, the walnut is not a nut, but a stone fruit. Like cherries and plums, walnuts have three layers, an outer skin, a fleshy layer, and a stone kernel (pit) in the center. But unlike the kernels of cherries and plums, we can break

Bananas come from South-East Asia and were known in prehistoric times.

Cherries, like plums and peaches, are stone fruits. Walnuts also belong to this group.

The pineapple belongs to the pseudocarps, or false fruits, and is native to the tropical part of America. Pineapples weighing 13 kg/28½ lb are said to have been grown in Brazil.

The lemon is one of the most important sources of vitamin C.

Bilberries, blackcurrants and gooseberries are all true berries. Blackberries and strawberries are not; the strawberry is a pseudocarp, and the blackberry is a multiple fruit.

The pear is a fruit with a core.

Exotic fruits: where they originally came from and what they taste like.

Fruit	Native country of origin	Taste
Avocado	Tropics	slightly nutty
Kiwifruit	New Zealand	sweet and sharp, a little like a gooseberry
Lychee	China	sweet, rose-like
Mango	East Asia	peach-like
Papaya	Middle America	melon-like
Passion fruit	South America	sweet and sharp
Tamarillo	Peru	sharpish, tomato-like

fruit weigh?

open this nut and eat the seed. In berries, all three layers are fleshy. The same applies to the cucumber, which is not a vegetable but a type of a berry fruit like the gooseberry or the blackcurrant. Blackberries and raspberries are called berries, but they are not really. They are called multiple fruits because many fruits form from one blossom. This gives them their clustered appearance. Even the strawberry isn't really a berry, but a pseudocarp, or false fruit. The real fruits are the 'seeds' which are partly embedded in the flesh.

There are fatty and non-fatty fruits. The flesh of the avocado pear gives the impression of being 'fat' and heavy, whereas a cucumber is crisp, watery and light. The avocado has the highest calorie content (163 cals per 100 g/3 oz) of any fruit that is eaten raw. The cucumber has the lowest, which is only about a tenth of the avocado (16 cals per 100 g/3 oz). More important than the calories are the vitamins in the fruit. If the body is deprived of certain vitamins over a long period of time deficiency illnesses can result. Scurvy, caused by vitamin C deficiency, used to be a very common disease on sailing ships. Citrus fruits such as lemons and oranges are high in vitamin C, and so are potatoes, peppers, green vegetables, rosehips and tomatoes. Tomatoes also contain a lot of vitamin A (also found in cod-liver oil, egg yolk, spinach, butter and carrots). Too little vitamin A can cause night-blindness or skin problems. Fruit is a source of vitamin B_1, (which is also found in fresh vegetables, wholemeal bread, yeast and liver). A lack of this vitamin can cause neuritis, or inflammation of the nerves.

An important vitamin for children is vitamin B_2, which regulates cell formation and promotes growth. Nuts are high in this vitamin, (which is also found in yeast, liver and wholemeal bread). Pantothenic acid regulates the metabolism and is essential for cell growth. It is found in fruit, as well as in eggs, milk, yeast and meat. Vitamin E is also important, and a lack of it can lead to muscle regression. It is found in peanuts, wheatgerm oil and soya beans.

Daily vitamin requirements for adults and children (in mg and µg)**

Vitamin	Adults	Children (7–9 years)
Vitamin A	0.9 mg	0.8 mg
Vitamin D	2.5 µg	2.5 µg
Vitamin E	12.0 mg	8 mg
Vitamin B_1	1.4–1.6 mg	1.2 mg
Vitamin B_2	1.8–2 mg	1.6 mg
Vitamin B_6	1.6–1.8 mg	1.4 mg
Niacin	9.0–15 mg	14 mg
Folic acid	400 mg	300 mg
Pantothenic acid	8 mg	6 mg
Vitamin C	75 mg	70 mg

**mg = milligram = a thousandth of a gram or 0.015 grains
µg = a millionth of a gram or 0.000015 grains

The pumpkin is a vegetable fruit. Some huge pumpkins have been grown. One giant example in the USA weighed in at a grand 277.6 kg/610 lb. In contrast, a 12-year-old child weighs about 40 kg/88 lb. It would need seven children to balance the weight of the enormous pumpkin!

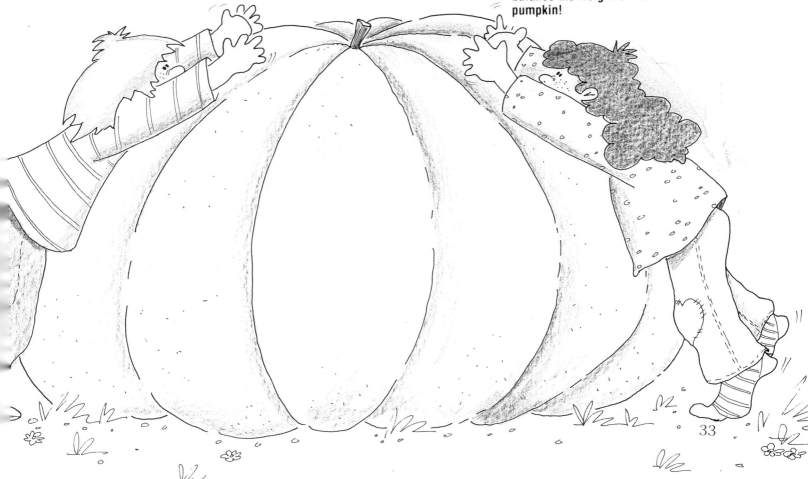

Why do plants and animals

The world loses on average one or more species of plant or animal every day. There are about 25,000 plants and more than 1000 animals (not including insects) which are threatened with extinction. This is mostly caused by the destruction of their natural habitat by man, but also because some species – seals or elephants, for instance – are hunted for their skins or their tusks, while others are captured to put in zoos or sell as exotic pets. In 1973, over 70 nations agreed to a convention which would attempt to stop these practices, and it is now illegal to trade in many of these threatened species.

Snowy owl

In Britain there are more than 30,000 species of animals and 5000 species of plants, but many of these are now protected by law, as they are in danger of dying out. The Wildlife and Countryside Act of 1981 was the most comprehensive wildlife law ever introduced in Britain, and there are heavy fines for people who offend against this. In the United States, the Endangered Species Act of 1973 protects rare wildlife from being hunted, collected, or otherwise threatened.

It is illegal in Britain to uproot any plant at all. Specially protected plants must not be picked or sold, nor may you collect their flowers or seeds. It is not against the law to pick non-protected wild flowers or fruit such as blackberries, but you should always leave enough for them to seed themselves and for others to enjoy.

The Californian condor, weighing 9 kg/20 lb and with a wingspan of 3 meters/9 feet, is also in grave danger of extinction. There are only 25 of these birds still in existence, and all of them are now in captivity. Biologists are trying to get them to breed in captivity to prevent the species from dying out altogether. It is hoped that, when the environmental problems which caused them to die out are solved, they will again be released into the wild.

It is not just preventing the animals and plants from being killed that is important – we must also protect their homes or nests. Killing, injuring, taking or selling specially protected wild animals such as the otter, badger and red squirrel is against the law, and disturbing them in their places of shelter is also illegal. In Britain, all wild birds, their nests and eggs are protected, except for 13 birds which are classed as pests, such as jackdaws, magpies and wood pigeons, and a few birds which may be shot for sport or for

food. There are Wildfowl Trusts which provide a protected natural habitat where the rarer birds can live and breed in safety. Pelican Island, in Florida, was the USA's first wildlife refuge, and Yellowstone National Park, established in 1872, was the world's first national park.

Specially protected animals include:

Badger	Bat
Dolphin	Great crested newt
Common porpoise	Red squirrel
Grizzly bear	Swallowtail butterfly
Large blue butterfly	Otter

With luck and the skill of the zoologists, the Californian condor may one day live and breed in the wild again.

There are more than 1200 national parks, wildlife reserves and similar protected areas throughout the world. In Britain, some wildlife areas are owned or managed by the Nature Conservancy Council as nature reserves. There were over 200 of these by 1985. They vary in size, but they are usually on land that has suffered little disturbance by man. They are left in their natural state and act as breeding reserves for various species which are in danger of extinction. The public is allowed to visit many of them, but they are not allowed to pick any wild flowers. In the United States, there are more than 80 sanctuaries which enclose very large feeding grounds for birds and other animals. National Parks are larger than reserves and sanctuaries. There are 10 of these in England and Wales, accounting for about 10 per cent of the total land area. They are intended for the public to enjoy, and there is often provision for camping, with footpaths, nature trails, and information centers. Protection of the landscape involves the preservation and planting of trees, clearing of derelict sites, and careful planning of any development within the Park.

National Parks in the USA, although set up mainly to preserve scenic features such as mountains, waterfalls, geysers, canyons and volcanic formations, also serve as refuges for the wild animals that live there, often in very wild countryside indeed.

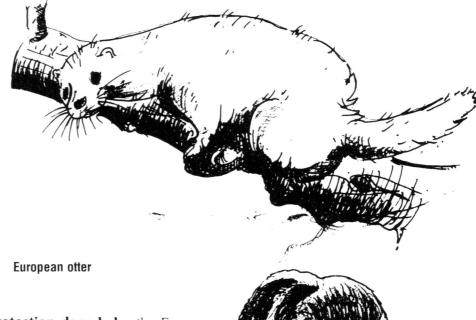

European otter

Protection does help: the European otter, which was dying out, is now increasing again slowly in Wales and the West of England. Pine martens, once widespread throughout Britain, are now only found in North-West Scotland, Northern England and North Wales, but they have recently been made a protected species, as have dormice. The grizzly bear, a large, ferocious animal that needs extensive wilderness to survive, would probably have died out by now were it not for the protected habitat of the Yellowstone National Park in the USA.

The grizzly bear still lives in the heart of Yellowstone National Park. With its great size and strength, it can kill a steer or bull with one blow of its paw.

Swallowtail butterfly

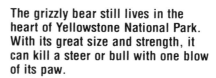

Specially protected plants include:	
Alpine gentian	Drooping saxifrage
Early spider orchid	Lady's slipper
Purple splurge	Spring gentian

There are special rules regarding bats, which apply everywhere except for the living areas in your home. You are not allowed to do anything that might harm bats found anywhere else, such as in your attic. Householders who have bats in their attics are even prevented from treating roof timbers with wood preservatives in case the bats are killed. As their natural roosts in hollow trees and caves have mostly disappeared, 90 per cent of bats now roost in buildings.

Bats have more rights to your home than you think!

Wild birds specially protected at all times include:	
Barn owl	Kingfisher
Bearded tit	Osprey
Bewick's swan	Peregrine falcon
Chough	Snowy owl
Whooper swan	Crossbills
Golden eagle	Californian condor

How long do trees live?

Trees are fascinating forms of life. Not only do they live a very long time, often becoming gigantic, but they also provide us with wood, fruit, and oxygen. Oxygen in the air is essential for all living things to breathe. This is how the tree produces it. Carbon dioxide is absorbed from the air through the tree's leaves. In the leaves is a green substance called chlorophyll, which works with energy from sunlight to convert the carbon dioxide into oxygen and also to form glucose which the tree absorbs as food. Without trees there would be no oxygen.

This tree is about 50 years old. You can tell that from its annual rings. You can also learn a lot of other things from the rings. You can tell when the tree grew quickly and when it grew slowly by looking at the spacing of the rings. Trees grow well when they have enough light, water and room, and they are in the right situation. A tree which grows well all the time has widely-spaced, even, annual rings. When there are long, dry spells, trees grow more slowly and the annual rings are closer together. Parasites also leave their mark. The rings are very narrow when a tree has been attacked by parasites. Trees do not thrive when they are too close together. As soon as neighboring trees are felled or die, the trees that are left grow faster. They will have narrow annual rings for the years of poor growth and wider ones to show the improved conditions later.

Some trees and bushes are evergreen, which means that they do not lose their leaves in winter. The leaves do die and fall off, but they do so gradually all through the year.

How long do the leaves of evergreen trees live?	
Ivy	1–2¼ years
Cranberry	2 years
Pine	2–3 years
Holly	2–4 years
Redwood	2–4 years
Swiss stone pine	2–6 years
Spruce	3–5 years
Laurel	4 years
Juniper	4–5 years
Fir	5–10 years
Mountain pine	5–13 years
Norfolk Island pine	15 years

How tall are trees when they are 10 years old?	m/ft
Maple, larch	4/13
Pine, spruce	2/6.5
Fir, Swiss stone pine, yew	1/3.25
Birch, alder, ash	over 4/13
Oak, lime, elm, copper beech, hornbeam	3/10

Good, sunny years with plenty of rainfall allow the tree to grow evenly and quickly. Its annual rings are widely-spaced and clearly defined.

The tree was attacked by parasites, as can be seen by the narrow annual rings.

At the beginning of its life, the tree had to find its way past a stone. In order to get a good hold in the ground, it developed more on the side away from the stone, and less where the stone pushed against it.

A forest fire damaged the tree. Its bark was burnt, but the tree survived, and its 'wounds' healed. The following year, new wood grew across the wound. The tree continued to grow undisturbed, as can be seen from the evenly-spaced annual rings.

During these years, there were possibly very hot, dry summers and not much rain in the winters either. When the annual rings lie very close to one another, it is a sign of long periods of drought.

Trees

How long do trees live?

	years		years
Rowan	80	Pine	500
Elder	100	Elm	500
Magnolia	100	Larch	600
Birch	120	Austrian pine	600
Holly	120	Norway maple	600
Hornbeam	150	Sweet chestnut	700
Willow	150	Olive	700
Aspen	150	Fir	800
Apple	200	Copper beech	900
Sycamore	200	Lime	900–1000
Pear	300	Spruce	1000
Ash	300	Oak	1200
Poplar	300	Cedar of Lebanon	1200–1300
Cherry	400	Plane	1300
Walnut	400	Redwood	3500

How tall do trees grow?

	m/ft
Juniper	15/49
Baobab (monkey bread)	18/59
Walnut	20/65
Tree-fern	22/72
Sweet chestnut	25/82
Birch	25/82
Horse chestnut	30/98
Ash	30/98
Plane	30/98
Coconut palm	32/104
Copper beech	44/144
Pine	48/157
Pedunculate oak	50/164
Cypress	52/170
Larch	53/173
Spruce	60/195
Fir	75/146
Douglas fir	127/416
Redwood	132/432
Giant eucalyptus	152/498

How wide do tree trunks get?

	m/ft	ins
Common maple	0.7/2	4
Birch	0.8/2	2
Juniper	0.9/2	10
Hornbeam	1/3	6
Pine	1/3	6
Larch	1.6/5	6
Ash	1.7/5	2
Spruce	2/6	2
Copper beech	2/6	2
Fir	3/9	9½
Elm	3/9	9½
Norway maple	3/9	9½
White poplar	4.5/14	8½
Yew	4.9/16	
Oak	7/22	
Sweet chestnut	8/26	
Redwood	11/36	
Baobab	15/49	

Trees do not grow at the same rate throughout their lifetime. Some, like the alder and pine, grow fast to begin with, then slow down. Others, such as the fir, grow faster after 20 years.

Annual growth of trees (in cm/in)

	1–20th year	21–40th year	41–60th year	61–80th year	81–100th year
Fir	12.5/5	54/21	48/18½	27.5/11	20/8
Spruce	30.5/12	48/18	38/15	25/10	16/6
Pine	44.5/17	40/15½	27/10½	19/7½	19/7½
Beech	27.5/10½	40.5/16	34/13	27/10½	14/5½
Oak	46.5/18	45/17½	29.5/11½	19.5/7½	17/6½
Alder	72.5/28	32/12	16/6	7/2½	–

A tree needs water as well as carbon dioxide to survive. In the course of a single summer, a birch tree will drink about 7000 liters/14,700 pints of water, and a 100-year-old birch tree will drink about 9000 liters/18,900 pints. The trees do not just 'drink' the water. A certain amount of it evaporates back into the air. About 50 liters/105 pints, evaporates from a beech and from a birch about 70 liters/147 pints.

Which are the largest birds?

Birds have to be fairly light to be able to fly. The pterodactyl *Quetzalcoatlus uorthropi*, which has been extinct for thousands of years, was the heaviest bird ever which was able to fly. It had a wingspan of over 15 meters/50 feet – as wide as ten 12-year-old children lying head to toe in a long line! Yet the pterodactyl weighed only 60 kg/132 lb – less than two 12-year-olds.

Two brainwaves of Nature enable birds to fly. Firstly, their bones are not solid. Some are hollow, and others are full of tiny empty spaces. This means that the bird is extremely light. Secondly, the lungs of most birds have air cells which extend into the entrails and the bones. They act like bellows, and are pumped up by the chest muscles of the bird whenever it is flying. A bird's feathers are designed to help it fly through the air. Massive chest muscles move its wings up and down. Some birds cannot fly because they are too heavy. Ostriches, penguins, emus and rheas are examples of flightless birds.

The largest bird today is the ostrich. The males grow to more than 2.7 meters/8 feet 9½ inches high – as tall as a 12-year-old child standing on the shoulders of an adult. Ostriches are far too heavy to fly. They weigh more than 150 kg/330 lb. An average 12-year-old child weighs 35 kg/77 lb, so an ostrich weighs more than four 12-year-olds! The African ostrich is found in the Sudan and in Ethiopia. At the other end of the scale, is the tiny bee humming-bird of Cuba. The adult bird is only 60 mm/2½ inches high, weighs 2 g/ .07 oz, and is smaller than some butterflies.

The ostrich can run at up to 72 kph/45 mph – as fast as a common hare, and slightly faster than a racing horse (70 kph/43 mph). Some birds fly faster than others. Compared with the fast fliers, the barn swallow seems a slowcoach at 60 kph/37.5 mph, but this is as fast as someone riding a moped flat out.

How far can birds fly without a break? Small birds can fly 400–500 km/250–310 miles without stopping. Even a tiny warbler can fly for 10 hours before getting tired. Large birds can fly much further – they can manage up to 1000 km/625 miles without a break. Birds which migrate (fly to warmer countries for the winter) have to cover huge distances.

The bird with the greatest wing-span is the wandering albatross – when its wings are outstretched, they measure 350 cm/136 inches from tip to tip. The same as three children in a line with arms outstretched and fingertips touching.

Wingspans	cm/in
White-tailed eagle	225/87½
Hawk	100–120/39–46
Stork	200/78
Heron	170/66
Crane	240/93½
Lapwing	75/29
Oystercatcher	82/31¾
Moorhen	55/21½
Black-headed gull	95/37
Herring gull	140/54½
Pelican	260/101
Mallard	90/35
Eider duck	105/40¾
Graylag goose	165/64
Trumpeter swan	300/117

A bird's flying speed does not necessarily depend on how large its wings are. Small birds can fly just as fast as big ones but they have to flap their wings more often:

Top flight speeds	kph/mph
Peregrine falcon	362/226
Golden eagle	240/150
Eider duck	113/70
Swift	92/57
House martin	80/50
Royal albatross	79/49

Compare the different shapes of birds in flight.

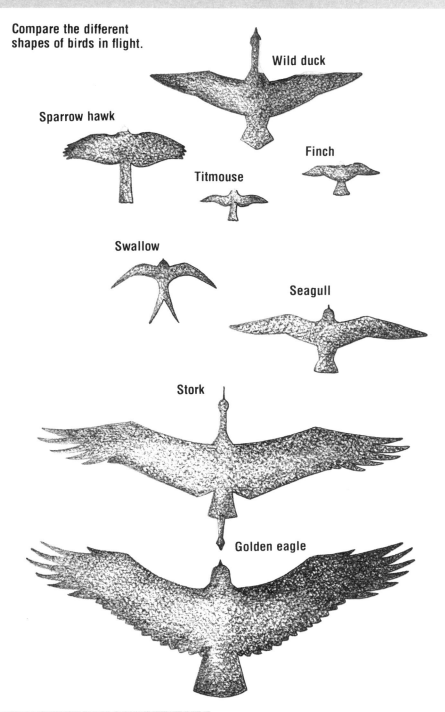

Wild duck

Sparrow hawk

Finch

Titmouse

Swallow

Seagull

Stork

Golden eagle

The top flight speed of a bird is not necessarily the speed at which it flies in formation, or in a flock. This is usually considerably slower. The flying height of different birds also varies a great deal.

	Flight speed kmh/ mph	Flying height m/ft		Flight speed kmh/ mph	Flying height m/ft
Titmouse	40/25	100/328	Crossbill	60/37	400/1312
Jackdaw	60/37	400/1312	Sparrow hawk	41/25	400/1312
Black-headed gull	50/31	400/1312	Starling	74/46	400/1312
Chaffinch	52/32	30/984	Peregrine falcon	60/37	400/1312
Barn swallow	44/27	400/1312	Lark	35–50/ 21–31	880/2886

A kite seems to fly high in the sky, yet the string of a kite is not more than 100 meters/330 feet long. The maximum height which most birds fly at is about 2000 meters/6560 feet, though eagles sometimes fly as high as 3000 meters/9840 feet. In the Andes and the Himalayas, condors and hawks occasionally fly as high as 7000 meters/22,950 feet above sea-level. Scientists think, however, that rising air currents help them to reach these great heights.

How fast can fish swim?

Fish cannot live out of water because they cannot breathe in air. Like all living creatures, they need oxygen to survive. Clean water contains oxygen which fish breathe in through their gills. The gills lie under the gill covers on the fish's head. They are tiny membranes which filter oxygen from the water. To do this, the gills must be able to move freely. When the fish is swimming, the gill covers open and water streams over the surface of the gills and keeps the membranes moving freely. When the fish is out of water, the gills stick together and it gasps for air because it cannot get enough oxygen.

When do fish spawn?

Most fish lay eggs; only a very few give birth to live young. The eggs and the sperm are both produced underwater and are brought together for fertilization by the movement of the water. This may sound rather chancy, but it is fact remarkably efficient. A few fish lay more

	No. of eggs
Herring	100,000
Catfish	60,000
Trout	1500–2000
Stickleback	80–100

than 100,000 eggs. The carp, for example, lays between 200,000 and 700,000. Other fish lay considerably fewer than this.

Fish do not all spawn at the same time. Some, like the stickleback, spawn in the spring, whereas others prefer winter.

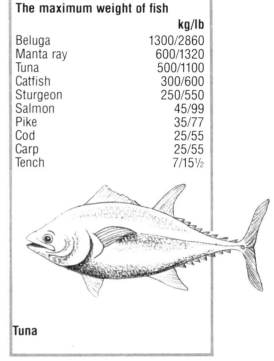

The maximum weight of fish	
	kg/lb
Beluga	1300/2860
Manta ray	600/1320
Tuna	500/1100
Catfish	300/600
Sturgeon	250/550
Salmon	45/99
Pike	35/77
Cod	25/55
Carp	25/55
Tench	7/15½

Tuna

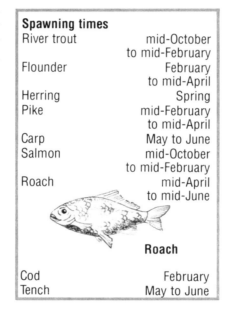

Spawning times	
River trout	mid-October to mid-February
Flounder	February to mid-April
Herring	Spring
Pike	mid-February to mid-April
Carp	May to June
Salmon	mid-October to mid-February
Roach	mid-April to mid-June

Roach

Cod	February
Tench	May to June

Compared with fish, man does not do very well in the water. He can only swim at 5–8 kph/3–5 mph.

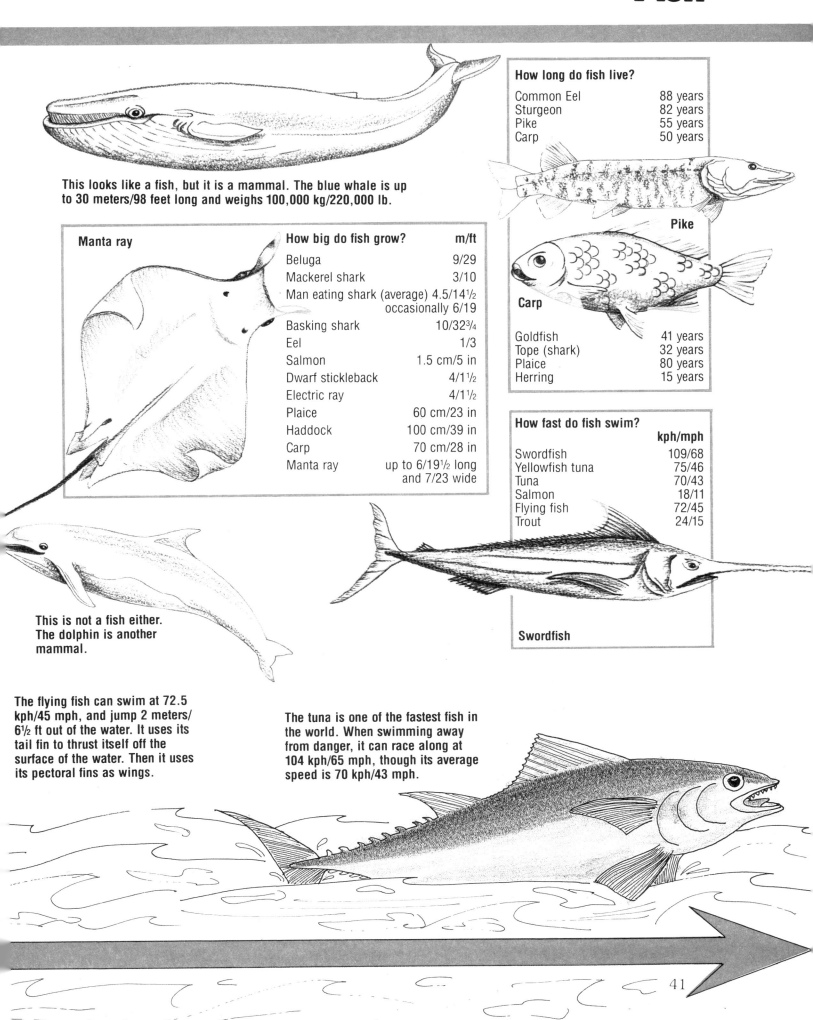

Fish

This looks like a fish, but it is a mammal. The blue whale is up to 30 meters/98 feet long and weighs 100,000 kg/220,000 lb.

How long do fish live?

Common Eel	88 years
Sturgeon	82 years
Pike	55 years
Carp	50 years

Pike

Carp

Goldfish	41 years
Tope (shark)	32 years
Plaice	80 years
Herring	15 years

Manta ray

How big do fish grow?

	m/ft
Beluga	9/29
Mackerel shark	3/10
Man eating shark (average)	4.5/14½
occasionally	6/19
Basking shark	10/32¾
Eel	1/3
Salmon	1.5 cm/5 in
Dwarf stickleback	4/1½
Electric ray	4/1½
Plaice	60 cm/23 in
Haddock	100 cm/39 in
Carp	70 cm/28 in
Manta ray	up to 6/19½ long and 7/23 wide

How fast do fish swim?

	kph/mph
Swordfish	109/68
Yellowfish tuna	75/46
Tuna	70/43
Salmon	18/11
Flying fish	72/45
Trout	24/15

Swordfish

This is not a fish either. The dolphin is another mammal.

The flying fish can swim at 72.5 kph/45 mph, and jump 2 meters/ 6½ ft out of the water. It uses its tail fin to thrust itself off the surface of the water. Then it uses its pectoral fins as wings.

The tuna is one of the fastest fish in the world. When swimming away from danger, it can race along at 104 kph/65 mph, though its average speed is 70 kph/43 mph.

Which is older, man or beast?

Dinosaurs lived from about 225 million years ago until roughly 65 million years ago. Then the largest living beings ever to walk the earth died out. This means that they are at least 63 million years older than the first 'real' man. The first 'real' man was *Homo habilis* or Handyman, who lived about 2 million years ago.

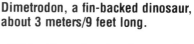

Dimetrodon, a fin-backed dinosaur, about 3 meters/9 feet long.

No one really knows why the dinosaurs died out. Scientists assume it had something to do with the great climactic changes which happened about 200 million years ago. Gigantic meteorites are supposed to have hit the earth and sent up huge quantities of dust. Possibly this dust caused a sudden alteration in the weather, with temperatures as cold as those in the Arctic today. Hardly any living thing, plant or animal, could survive this cold.

There were flesh-eating and plant-eating dinosaurs. The flesh-eating ones (theropods) stood and moved on their hind legs. The plant-eaters (sauropods) mostly had long necks and walked on all fours. There were also enormous pterodactyls (pterosaurs), and marine reptiles (ichthyosaurs). Most dinosaur skeletons have been found in North America, East Africa and Middle Asia, and dinosaur eggs have even been found in the Gobi desert.

In 1932, American scientists were extremely surprised to discover the fossilized tracks of an enormous animal in Salt Lake City (USA). It was the footprint of a bipedal (two-footed) hadrosaurus, and was 1.36 meters/4½ feet long and 82 cm/31 inches wide. A small child could happily have had a swim in this monster footstep. In 1979, scientists found the bones of another huge dinosaur, the brachiosaurus, in the Dry Mesa Quarry in Wyoming (USA). Its shoulder blades alone are 2.7 meters/9 feet long. It weighed 40 tonnes, which is as heavy as 10 fully-grown elephants. The barosaurus was also huge – 44 meters/144 feet from head to tail. There were smaller dinosaurs, however. According to footprints found in Nova Scotia (Canada), one species was only as big as a sparrow.

The barosaurus – a real 'super-saurus' – was one of the diplodocus family. You can get an idea of its enormous size if you imagine it eating the flowers in the top windowboxes of a three-storeyed house, which it could easily have done. Barosaurus lived 160 million years ago in the USA. Its cousin, Diplodocus carnegii, was not exactly tiny, either. It measured 26 meters/

85 feet from head to foot, and its tail alone was 15 meters/44 feet long. Scientists do not think that diplodocus was particularly heavy, however. It weighed about 5 tonnes, which is as heavy as two hippopotamuses. Diplodocus was found in Wyoming (USA) in 1899, and there is a life-size model of one in Pittsburg Museum.

Dinosaurs had small brains but the most stupid of them all was probably Stegosaurus. Its brain was the size of a walnut and weighed 70 g/2½ oz. A human brain is 21 times heavier than that (1200–1800 g/42–63 oz), and an elephant's brain is 71 times heavier (5000 g/176 oz). Stegosaurus was 9 meters/29 feet long and, at 1750 kg/ 3850 lb weighed as much as a rhinoceros. It lived 150 million years ago.

The biggest and most fearsome flesh-eating dinosaur was Tyrannosaurus Rex. It weighed 4.5 tonnes, making it slightly heavier than an elephant. When upright, it stood 5.6 meters/18 feet tall and it measured 10 meters/ 33 ft from head to tail. It lived about 75 million years ago.

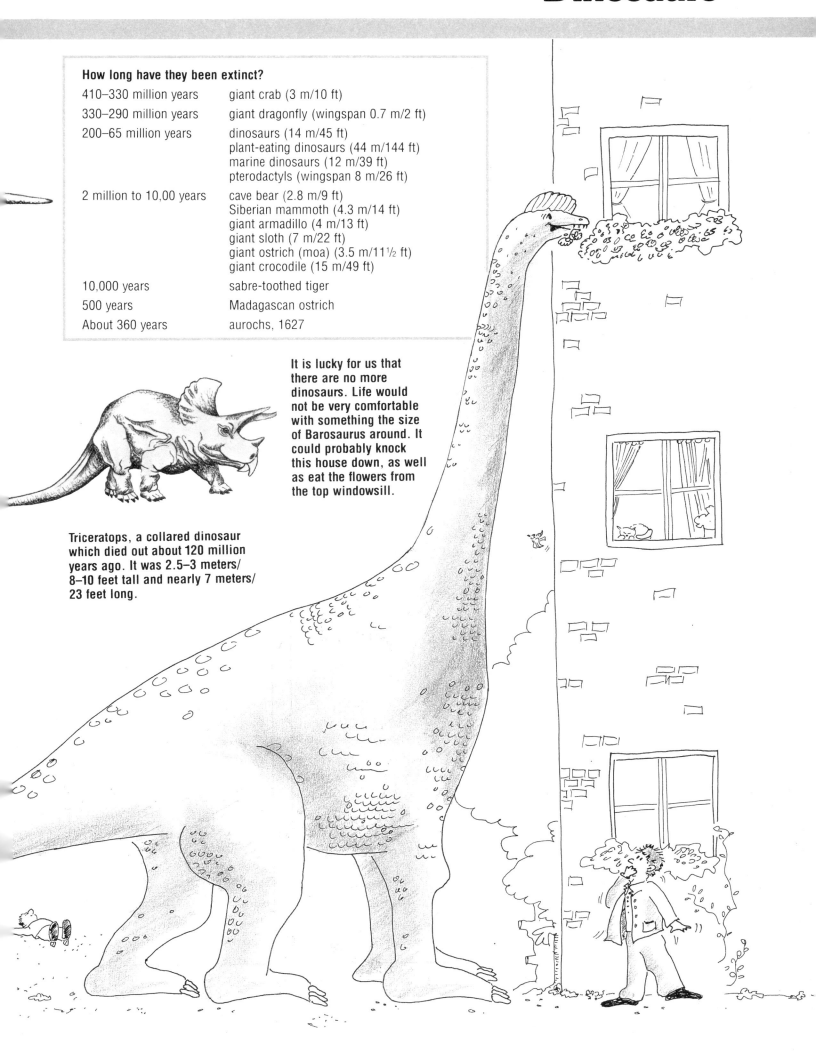

How long have they been extinct?

410–330 million years	giant crab (3 m/10 ft)
330–290 million years	giant dragonfly (wingspan 0.7 m/2 ft)
200–65 million years	dinosaurs (14 m/45 ft)
	plant-eating dinosaurs (44 m/144 ft)
	marine dinosaurs (12 m/39 ft)
	pterodactyls (wingspan 8 m/26 ft)
2 million to 10,00 years	cave bear (2.8 m/9 ft)
	Siberian mammoth (4.3 m/14 ft)
	giant armadillo (4 m/13 ft)
	giant sloth (7 m/22 ft)
	giant ostrich (moa) (3.5 m/11½ ft)
	giant crocodile (15 m/49 ft)
10,000 years	sabre-toothed tiger
500 years	Madagascan ostrich
About 360 years	aurochs, 1627

It is lucky for us that there are no more dinosaurs. Life would not be very comfortable with something the size of Barosaurus around. It could probably knock this house down, as well as eat the flowers from the top windowsill.

Triceratops, a collared dinosaur which died out about 120 million years ago. It was 2.5–3 meters/ 8–10 feet tall and nearly 7 meters/ 23 feet long.

How big do snakes grow?

Reptiles are descended from the dinosaurs. Turtles, tortoises, lizards, crocodiles and snakes are all reptiles. They have certain characteristics in common: they breathe with lungs and have skeletons, and their bodies are covered with scales or, as in the case of tortoises and turtles, with a shell.

All reptiles develop inside their eggs. Some reptiles, such as turtles, lay these eggs before the young have hatched. Others carry the eggs in their bodies and do not give birth until the young reptiles are fully developed and hatch from the egg inside the mother. It looks as if the mothers give birth to live offspring, but they are inside eggs until they are ready to be born.

Reptiles can grow fairly large, but never as big as their ancestors, the dinosaurs. The snakes are the longest reptiles. The longest and heaviest snake is the anaconda, which grows to more than 8 meters/26 feet long. Some are supposed to have reached 9 meters/29 feet, but there is no proof that these measurements are accurate. The reticulated pythons are also enormous – fully-grown, they are at least 6 meters/19 feet long, and sometimes over 9 meters/29 feet. So both of these snakes are nearly as long as three family cars. Neither of them is found in Europe, however, and the European snakes are not nearly as large. The common adder, found in Europe and Asia, grows to a maximum of 80 cm/30 inches, and it is usually gray with a black zigzag band on the back. Its bite is rarely fatal to man.

Reptiles can live to a great age	
Marion's tortoise from Seychelles	152 years
Mediterranean spur-thighed tortoise	116 years
Mississippi alligator	66 years
Blindworm	54 years
Japanese giant salamander	51 years
Green turtle	50 years
Boa constrictor	40 years

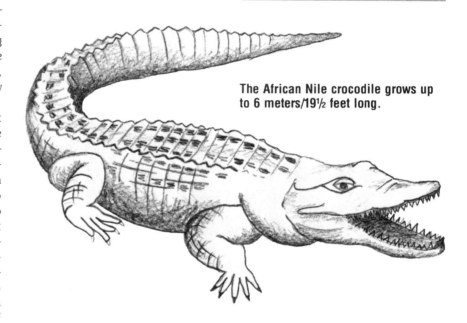

The African Nile crocodile grows up to 6 meters/19½ feet long.

How long are snakes?			
Anaconda	8.45 m/27½ ft	Black mamba	2.1 m/7 ft
Reticulated python	6–10 m/ 19–32 ft	Grass snake	100 cm/39 in
		Common adder	80 cm/30 in
Diamondback rattlesnake	2.3 m/ 7½ ft	Dwarf puff adder	23 cm/9 in
King cobra	5.5–5.7 m/18–18½ ft	The smallest snake in the world is the very rare thread snake known only in	
Boa constrictor	4.3 m/14ft	the West Indies	10.8 cm/4¼ in

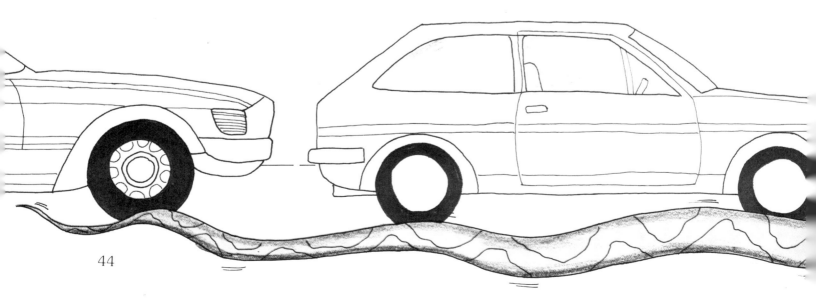

The common tortoise is tiny compared with leatherback turtles.

Leatherbacks are the largest turtles. They are about 2 meters/ 6½ feet long and weigh up to 600 kg/1320 lb. A giant example has been caught. It was 2.54 meters/8 feet long and weighed 1883 lb. Leatherbacks live in the Pacific Ocean. The largest tortoise, *Geochelone giganthea* is found near Madagascar on an island in the Indian Ocean. It weighs over 250 kg/550 lb. The common tortoise is quite small. It grows to about 18–25 cm/7–10 inches long.

The monitor lizards are amongst the largest lizards. These dragon-like reptiles are not only big, but dangerous as well. The Nile monitor in Africa even preys on young crocodiles. All monitor lizards are predatory and eggs of any shape or size are amongst their favorite delicacies. The Komodo dragon, which lives in Indonesia and is the largest lizard of all, grows to a length of 3 meters/10 feet and can weigh up to 135 kg/30 lb. It can also live to be 100 years old. The two-banded or water monitor lives in South-east Asia and grows to 2.7 meters/ 9 feet. Blind-worms are related to lizards. Although they look like small snakes, they have the stunted remains of legs underneath their skin.

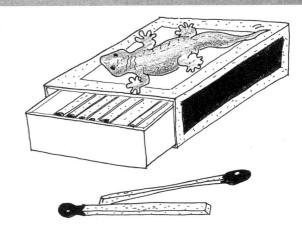

The smallest reptile on earth is the gecko *Spaerodactylus*, which is smaller than a matchbox. It grows to only 36 mm/1¼ inches in length, of which half is body and the other half tail. These particular geckos are only found on one of the Virgin Islands in the Caribbean.

Reticulated pythons and anacondas are record-holders for being the longest snakes. When fully-grown, they are both nearly as long as three family cars parked one behind the other. One snake can produce up to 45 youngsters at once, as a boa constrictor in the zoo in Donai La Fontaine in France did. The young snakes on this record-breaking occasion were 30 cm/11½ inches long, and the mother was 2.5 meters/8 feet, weighing 8 kg/17½ lb.

Be careful when a giant chameleon sticks its tongue out at you! It is nearly 5 meters/16 feet long. If you compare that with the pages of this book, the chameleon's tongue would cover 23 pages spread out in a row.

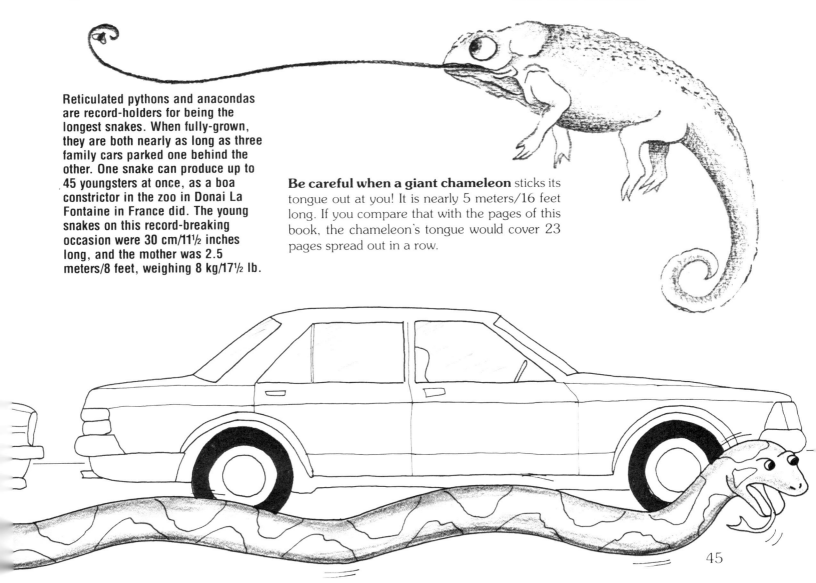

Which plants and animals are

Monkshood

Foxglove

Poisons are not always fatal. Some snake venom does not take effect for several hours, giving an opportunity to do something about it. Others are not actually deadly, but cause very serious illness in people or animals. Certain poisons are not toxic when taken in small quantities. Cooking salt, alcohol and cigarette nicotine are examples. It is when people use them too much or they become a habit that they damage health. Many poisons are present in plants – in some toadstools, for example, or in the plant nux vomica, from which strychnine, a very dangerous poison, comes. The South American Jivaro Indians use nux vomica to prepare the poison for their poisoned arrows.

Many mushrooms and toadstools are poisonous, and some are deadly. The yellowish-olive Death Cap is regarded as the world's most poisonous fungus. It is found in Europe and North America. The fly agaric and some morels are also dangerous and can be fatal. Poisonous fungi cause vomiting, delirium, stomach and calf pains, and sometimes collapse and death. The poison begins to work between six and 15 hours after tasting the fungus. You should call a doctor immediately if mushroom poisoning is suspected.

Zombies do exist. They are not like the ones in horror films, however, living corpses bringing destruction and disaster. The American ethnologist, Dr Edmond Wade, discovered zombies on Haiti, an island in the Caribbean. The people there believe in the voodoo cult, which is a mixture of religion, medicine, and magic. Voodoo witch doctors use various poisons to turn people into zombies as punishment for crimes or bad conduct.

First the condemned person is poisoned with a substance taken from the reproductive glands of the globefish. Even a small quantity of this poison is fatal to man but the witch doctors know how to prepare an amount that is not quite deadly, but has devastating effects. The condemned person cannot breathe, cannot move, loses consciousness, and appears to be dead.

This fools even the doctors, who pronounce the person dead. He is then buried. But the witch doctors can call him back to life again with the help of another drug made from a plant of the datura family. He begins to breathe again, and his heart beats regularly, but it is as if he is dazed or drunk. This is the intention, for he now becomes the slave of the witch doctors. He must pay for his crime for the rest of his life by working for them on the sugar cane plantations, in the quarries or in the mills. The zombie remains in a stupor which is maintained by poisons or drugs, and he is never allowed to return to his family.

Deadly nightshade

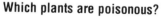

Which plants are poisonous?

Yew	Spurge
Laburnum	Laurel
Cuckoopint	Meadow saffron
Crowfoot	Water hemlock
Monkshood	Hemlock
Poppy	(US Poison hemlock)
Celandine	Thorn apple
Foxglove	(US Jimson weed)
Bryony	Deadly nightshade
Lobelia	

poisonous?

Which animals are poisonous?
It is hard to believe, but bees, wasps, bumblebees, ants and hornets count as poisonous. Their stings are painful, but only cause death when someone is stung many times at once. The brown spider, found in America and parts of Europe, has a bite which causes a stinging feeling or burning pain. This is followed by redness and blistering, and has very unpleasant effects which can sometimes lead to death. Most poisonous snakes live in hot parts of the world such as the tropics. The bite of the common adder or viper is rarely fatal, but anyone who is bitten should immediately go to hospital to be treated with snake serum.

Which of the poisonous animals are deadly to man?

	Where poison is found
Moray eel	in mucous membrane of palate
Rattlesnake	venom fang
Spectacled snake	venom fang
Sea snake	very small venom fangs
Cobra	venom fangs
Black mamba	venom fangs
Puff adder	venom fang
Common adder	venom fangs in upper jaw

The bite of another spider, the tarantula, is also very painful. Tarantulas are 25–37 mm/0.91–1¼ inches long and live in Southern Europe.

Scorpions live in all of the world's hot countries – Spain in Europe, for example. All scorpions are poisonous, but not necessarily deadly to man. The sting of the European scorpion is about as painful as a wasp sting. The sting of the scorpions found in tropical countries can sometimes be fatal.

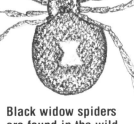

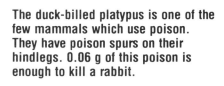

Of around 510 snake varieties in the world, 17 per cent are poisonous. Amongst them is the common adder. It inflicts a nasty bite but is rarely fatal.

Black widow spiders are found in the wild almost exclusively in America, where they are quite widespread. They bite with their poison fangs and this is always extremely painful, and sometimes deadly.

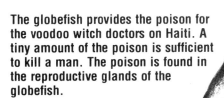

The globefish provides the poison for the voodoo witch doctors on Haiti. A tiny amount of the poison is sufficient to kill a man. The poison is found in the reproductive glands of the globefish.

The duck-billed platypus is one of the few mammals which use poison. They have poison spurs on their hindlegs. 0.06 g of this poison is enough to kill a rabbit.

47

How much can insects carry?

You may think that fleas jump, lice crawl and earwigs run about on the ground and you would be right. Scientifically speaking, however, all these insects belong to the family of flying insects, just as flies, bees, beetles, butterflies and grasshoppers do. It is said that flying insects are a more highly developed form of insect than insects which cannot fly, and have never possessed wings. Silverfish belong to this category, which is known as the primitive insects. They are small, gray, fish-like vermin which flit around in the home, and they can be found anywhere where it is dark and moist. Silverfish may not be very pretty, but at least they do no damage, unlike some insects.

Insects do not like living on their own. Some, like ants, build proper colonies. Termites and bees create whole states or populations. These insects have even developed their own 'languages'. Bees do a special dance at the hive to tell their fellows where food is to be found. Insects which build colonies have a sense of time and can find their bearings even in unknown territory, so the bee can use his 'talking dance' to tell the other bees which direction to fly in, and how long they have to fly before they find the food source.

Some insect colonies have only a few members, and others are vast. One type of wasp has only twelve wasps in a colony, whereas an ordinary wasps' nest has a few hundred wasps. The same goes for hornets. Bumblebees have colonies of 300–400 members, and certain types of wasp have colonies with up to 4000 members. Honeybees' colonies are five times as big as this, with 20,000–80,000 members. They are outdone only by ants and termites, who live together with a million friends under one roof.

The housefly can carry 1.7 times its own weight, but a man cannot carry as much as his own body weight. Only top athletes and men working in heavy industries are stronger.

Many insects are incredibly strong – far stronger than the strongest muscleman. Ants have been observed to carry stones weighing 52 times their own weight. In human terms, that would mean carrying about 4000 kg/8800 lb – about the weight of a fully-grown elephant. In fact, a man can only carry five-sixths of his own body weight. This is about 60 kg/132 lb, which is equivalent to a heavy sack of coal or potatoes. The rhinoceros beetle is capable of even greater feats of strength than the ant, it can carry 850 times its own weight – on its back. An elephant would have to carry a large freight ship on its back

How far can insects fly?			
Insect	**Flight distance (km/miles)**	**Insect**	**Flight distance (km/miles)**
Mosquito	32/20 (without a break)	Australian painted lady	1900/1187 (from Australia to New Zealand)
Butterfly	150/93 (without a break)	European painted lady	1800/1125 (from N. Africa to Middle Europe)

to equal the strength of a rhinoceros beetle. Bees can drag extraordinary loads. They can pull 300 times their own weight behind them. In human terms, that would mean a man pulling three lorries hitched together. Of course, not all insects are as strong as the ant or the rhinoceros beetle, but many insects are a great deal stronger than humans.

How fast can insects fly?

	m/ft per second
Grasshopper	15/49
Dragonfly	10/32
Gadfly	7/23
Bumblebee	3.5/11½
Housefly	1.8/6
Mosquito	1.5/5
Honeybee	3.7/12
Cockchafer	2.2/7
Dung-beetle	7/23

How often do insects beat their wings? (The smaller the insect, the more times it beats its wings)

	Wing beats per second
Cockroach	50
Bumblebee	200
Bee	250
Gnat	300
Chironomids (the tiny midges which swarm or dance over ponds)	600
Housefly	190
Grasshopper	35
Ladybug	90

If a child were as strong as an ant, he could carry an elephant.

Insect	Own weight	Greatest load	How many times own weight
	g	g	
Housefly	0.013	0.023	1.77
Grasshopper	0.1	1.6	16
Honeybee	0.085	0.065	0.76
Bumblebee	0.214	0.134	0.62
Bee	0.085	25	300

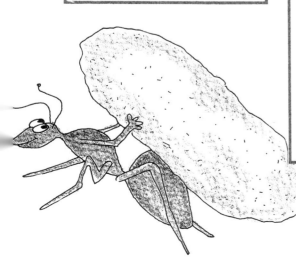

Ants can carry 52 times their own body weight.

How much does a person need

Our food contains energy. Our body cells convert the food into power, and in the process the energy is 'burnt' in the same way as fuel is burnt in an engine. So the energy content of food is calculated according to its calorific or 'fuel' value, and this is measured in calories, or units of heat. The abbreviation 'kcal' is used. This is short for kilocalorie (1 kilocalorie = 1000 calories). There is also another measuring system, joules (1 calorie = 4.2 joules). The amount a person needs to eat depends on his age and his occupation.

Energy used in various activities (in kcal per hour unless otherwise indicated)	
Lying down	20
Sitting	26
Standing	44
Driving (country roads)	60
Washing-up	152
Cycling (10 kph/6.25 mph)	168
Ironing	182
Walking (5 kph/3 mph)	188
Driving (town, rush hour)	192
Chopping wood	224
Weeding	266
Cross-country skiing (4 kph/2.5 mph)	480
Shoveling snow	500
Jogging (9 kph/5.6 mph)	600
Swimming (50 m/160 ft in a minute)	680

The important nutrients which the body needs are proteins, fats, carbohydrates, water, minerals and vitamins. Fats and carbohydrates are the main sources of energy. 1 g/0.28 oz of fat produces 9.3 kcal of energy. In comparison, 1 g/0.28 oz of carbohydrate produces only 4.1 kcal of energy.

A laborer on a building site needs a good 4000 kcal per day. In theory, he can provide this with 976 g/ 34¼ oz of carbohydrate, but he would need only 430 g/15 oz of pure fat for the same amount of energy. Protein is hardly ever converted into energy.

Protein is very necessary in the diet because it is vital building material. You can feed yourself well without having too many calories. 100 g/3½ oz of sausages contains 274 kcal, for example, but 100 g/ 3½ oz of cod contains only 76 kcal, which is less than a third. And yet cod contains more protein: 17.4 g/0.6 oz as opposed to the sausages which have only 9.5 g/0.3 oz.

Meals can be put together in all kinds of different ways. These two examples contain the same amount of energy, but the first menu would very soon cause deficiency symptoms if it was continued day after day. A glass of lemonade (100 kcal), 100 g/3½ oz of roasted peanuts (629 kcal) and a bar of chocolate (526 kcal) contain 1255 kcal in all. Instead of that, you could have three whole lettuces (60 kcal), a big lean steak (200 g/7 oz = 336 kcal), 300 g/10 oz of potatoes (220 kcal) 1 kg/2.2 lb of tomatoes (210 kcal), 600 g/21 oz of tinned pineapple and, as a final treat, a chocolate as well (100 kcal).

Most of our food is converted into heat in our bodies, and only a little of it is used for work. People who work hard need a lot of calories daily. A miner, a carpenter or a blacksmith need as much energy as a laborer. These people are amongst the 'heaviest' workers. Doctors, mechanics and sales assist-ants belong to the 'heavy' category, and they need a good 3000 kcal daily. 'Light' workers – officials and office workers – need about 2400 kcal per day, and a 75 year old grandmother needs 1800 kcal – the same as her five-year-old grandson.

Locusts are terrible gluttons. It has been calculated that a swarm of locusts, weighing 5000 tonnes and consisting of 1.6 billion creatures, can consume 50,000 tonnes of plant crops – 10 times their own weight. A large swarm of locusts uses as many calories every day as a city with 150,000 inhabitants. Think how much a child would have to eat, to keep up with a locust!

Nutrition

The harder you work, the more energy you use. But the body uses energy even when it is resting – just lying down uses 20 kcal per hour. A 200 g/7 oz apple contains 114 kcal, so if you lie down for six hours you use just over the amount of energy provided by an apple. If you go cross-country skiing at 4 kph/2¼ mph, you need 480 kcal, or more than four apples an hour. And swimming breaststroke at a rate of 50 meters/160 feet in one minute burns up the energy content of five apples.

Lying down uses 20 kcal an hour. Sitting is a little more strenuous – 26 kcal are burnt up by the body. More energy is needed for sweeping – about 155 kcal.

Nutritional values of some foods						
100 g/3½ oz contain	Calories (kcal)	Joule (kj)	Water (g/oz)	Protein (g/oz)	Fat (g/oz)	Carbo-hydrate (g/oz)
Roast chicken	133	559	73/2.5	21/0.7	6/0.2	–
Lean rump steak, grilled	174	731	68/2.4	20/0.7	–	–
Cod	76	319	82/2.8	17/0.6	0.7/0.02	–
Whole milk	64	269	87/3	3/0.1	5/0.17	4/0.2
Butter	754	3167	15/0.5	0.7/0.02	83/2.9	0.7/0.02
Potato crisps	582	2444	1.8/0.06	5.5/0.19	39/1.3	46/1.6
Lettuce	17	71	94/3.3	1.4/0.04	0.2/0.007	2.2/0.07
Apple	57	239	85/3	0.3/0.01	0.4/0.01	13/0.45
Banana	96	403	74/2.6	1.1/0.03	0.2/0.007	22/0.7
Tomato ketchup	104	437	68/2.4	2/0.07	–	24/0.84
Milk chocolate	526	2209	1/0.03	8/0.2	30/1	56/2
Roasted peanuts	629	2642	2/0.07	26/0.9	49/1.7	21/0.7
Jam	282	1284	29/1	0.6/0.02	–	70/2.4
Coffee	5	21	98/3.4	0.3/0.01	–	0.8/0.02
Tea	2	8.4	99/3.4	0.1/0.003	–	0.4/0.01
Lemonade	49	206	92/3.2	–	–	12/0.4

Who has the best tastebuds?

Many animals taste with their mouths, but there are some exceptions. An eel tastes with its skin, a fly with its feet, an octopus with the suckers on its tentacles. Fish and amphibians sometimes taste with their heads, and sometimes with their bodies, and a butterfly can detect an agreeable taste with his antennae. Mussels and snails cannot tell the difference between tasting and smelling. Even for human beings, taste and smell are very closely linked. We can actually only tell if something tastes sweet, sour, salty or bitter. All the other sensations of taste are in fact smell.

Humans have a very bad sense of taste compared with that of animals. We can hardly tell if a 1 g/ 0.28 oz of sugar is dissolved in ¼ liter/½ pint of water. Fish can tell if there is this amount of sugar in a hundred times that amount of water.

A fly can tell even if there is a 1 g/ 0.28 oz of sugar in 40 liters/84 pints of water. The star of the taste connoisseurs is the butterfly, which can tell if there is a trace of sugar in 300 liters/630 pints of water. That's the same as if you dissolved ⅕ of a sugar cube in a gigantic aquarium. Imagine being able to taste that!

Why does some food have a bitter aftertaste? Take a look at your tongue under a magnifying glass. It looks like a rough towel. On each of those 'knobs' there are up to about 100 tastebuds. The human mouth contains roughly 10,000 tastebuds in all, some for sweet, some for salty, some for sour, and some for bitter tastes. These different tastebuds are not distributed evenly throughout the mouth, but are grouped in certain areas of the tongue. You can taste sweet things on the tip of your tongue, sour things at the left and right of the tongue, salty things all round the edge of the tongue and bitter things right at the back. So you don't taste bitter things until the last minute, just as you are about to swallow the food. That is why some food seems to have a bitter aftertaste.

'Just you keep away from my water! There's nothing in it that you like!'

'What a rotten sense of taste you've got! There was fruit juice in that glass before, with sweet sugar. That's what I'm after.'

Who eats the most ice cream? The USA is the home of ice cream and Americans eat more of it than anyone else. On average, they get through 21 liters/44 pints each year. Runners-up for the title are Sweden 14.2 liters/29 pints, Denmark and Switzerland both 8 liters/16.8 pints. Funnily enough, people in the hotter countries don't eat so much. Spain has a consumption of only 2.8 liters/6 pints per head, and Portugal 1.7 liters/3.4 pints.

The food that we eat is digested in the stomach, but some kinds of food stay in the stomach longer than others. Certain foods are easily digestible. For example, honey only stays in the stomach for a few minutes. Others are hard to digest, such as sardines in oil which are still 'swimming around' seven or eight hours later. This table shows how long different foods stay in the stomach.

Time necessary to digest certain foods	
10 minutes:	Honey
1–2 hours:	Tea, coffee, soft-boiled egg, boiled milk
2–3 hours:	Coffee with cream, cocoa with milk, hard-boiled egg, scrambled egg, white fish, cauliflower, cherry jam, biscuits, white bread
3–4 hours:	Chicken meat, ham, beef, wholemeal bread, rice, carrots, spinach, cucumber, radishes, apples
4–5 hours:	Roast and smoked meats, kippers, lentils, runner beans
5–6 hours:	Bacon
6–7 hours:	Mushrooms, herrings in tomato sauce
7–8 hours:	Sardines in oil

The length of time food stays in the stomach also depends on the amount that is eaten: large portions take longer and make your stomach feel 'heavy'. If you eat small portions more often, your stomach feels lighter.

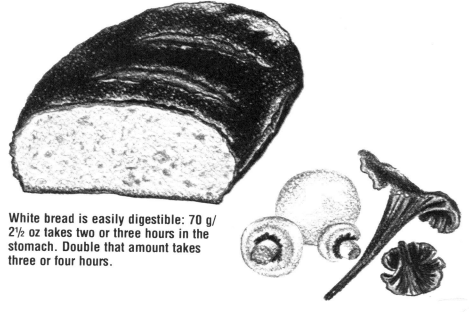

White bread is easily digestible: 70 g/ 2½ oz takes two or three hours in the stomach. Double that amount takes three or four hours.

Mushrooms are hard to digest. It is six or seven hours before they leave the stomach.

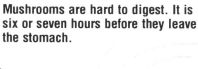

You can drink plenty of coffee and tea without milk or sugar, and after two hours it has all gone through your system, but coffee and tea with milk or sugar take one or two hours longer.

Cookies belong to the easily digested foodstuffs – they are in the stomach for two or three hours.

Strawberries stay in the stomach for three or four hours.

These should be left alone – sugar (and sweets are nearly all sugar) is admittedly easily digestible, but it is bad for your teeth and your figure.

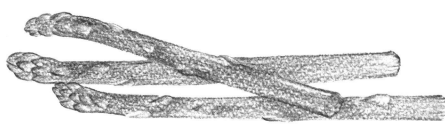

150 g/5 oz of asparagus doesn't stay in the stomach very long. It goes through to the intestine after two or three hours.

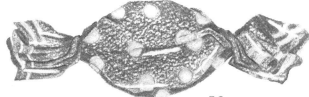

Who has the best hearing?

People have ears, and so have many animals, but ears vary in shape and size according to what they have to hear. Many animals hear far more with their ears than people do. Bats, dogs, cats, rats and mice can hear sounds which are far too high-pitched for us to hear (ultrasound). Other animals, such as the wood grouse, hear tones which are much too low for our ears (infrasound).

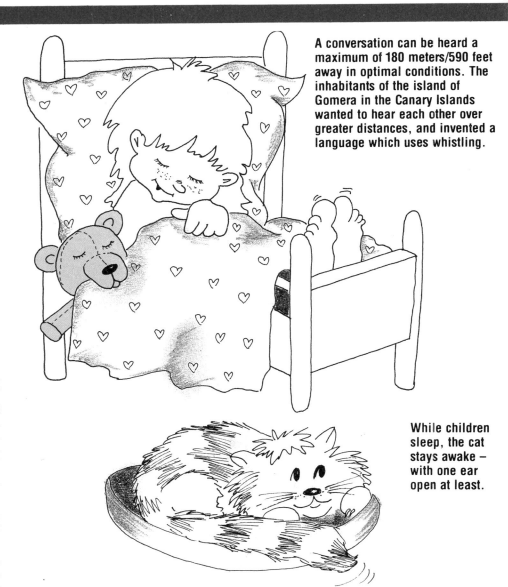

A conversation can be heard a maximum of 180 meters/590 feet away in optimal conditions. The inhabitants of the island of Gomera in the Canary Islands wanted to hear each other over greater distances, and invented a language which uses whistling.

While children sleep, the cat stays awake – with one ear open at least.

How are sounds formed and how can we understand them?

You can think of sounds as being like waves in water. The sound is formed by vibrations. When someone is speaking, the air is forced out of the lungs past the vocal chords. This creates vibrations or weak pressure waves, which are carried out into the air. Our ears react to these waves of pressure. You can think of an ear as being like a drum: pressure or beats on the drum cause it to vibrate. The drum corresponds to our eardrum. As sound, in the form of sound waves, hits the eardrum, it vibrates. These vibrations are transferred via the auditory nerves to the brain. This all occurs so fast that we are not even aware of it happening. The ear can distinguish between high and low sounds.

You can measure the number of vibrations a sound makes. Sound vibrations are measured in Hertz (Hz). A human being can hear sounds from 16 Hertz to about 20,000 Hertz. Sound vibrations below 16 Hertz are called infrasound, and those above 20,000 Hertz are ultrasound.

Children can hear better than adults. They can hear sounds above 20,000 Hertz, and children who suffer from asthma can hear sounds up to 30,000 Hertz. This is why children can hear bats squeaking, although they cannot distinguish between the higher and lower tones of these squeaks. Bat sounds or melodies can only be heard when recorded and played back at half speed.

While we sleep, things are not as quiet as they seem around us. Mice roam around, looking for food and meeting their friends. They make squeaky noises which we cannot hear (25,000–50,000 Hertz). But for their fellow mice, these little squeaks are extremely noisy. It is not only the mice who are disturbed. Cats, too, are woken by the noise, and look forward to their approaching mouse dinner.

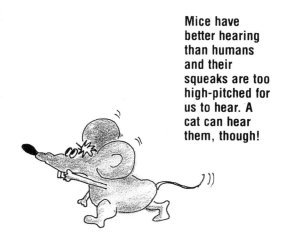

Mice have better hearing than humans and their squeaks are too high-pitched for us to hear. A cat can hear them, though!

Hearing

The volume of different sounds is measured in decibels (dB). All sounds which can only just be picked up by measuring apparatus are given the value 0 dB, and this is the sound threshold. It is a rather complicated business to work out the volume of a sound. Here are a few examples: if the sound intensity increases tenfold, the volume increases by 10 dB. If a typewriter has a volume of 50 dB, two typewriters would have a volume of 52 dB, 10 typewriters = 60 db, 100 typewriters = 70 dB, and 1000 typewriters = 80 dB. When a volume of 130 dB is reached, it hurts our ears, and this is known as the pain threshold. Your ears can be damaged by a volume of 140 dB, and permanent hearing loss can be caused by 150 dB. Volumes greater than 192 dB give a shock so great that they can cause death. This table shows some sounds and their value in decibels:

Bats 'see' with their ears, and they fly using a system of echo-location.

A deaf bat would not be able to survive, but a blind bat would manage very well indeed: bats fly using a system of echo-location, and they do not have to be able to see. They emit sounds that humans cannot hear. These echo-sounds bounce off obstructions or food sources, and return to the bat. The bat can even distinguish different kinds of insects depending on the kind of echo which is returned. Its brain sorts all this information in seconds, even though it is no bigger than a pinhead.

Volumes	dB
Hearing threshold	0
Well-insulated, soundproof room	10
Whispering	15
Broadcasting studio	20
Quiet residential street	30
Light traffic	40
Single typewriter	50
Conversation 1 m/ 3 ft away	60
Piano 3 m/10 ft away	70
Moped	80
Heavy lorry 7 m/ 23 ft away	85
Pneumatic drill, 10 m/ 33 ft away	95
Fire engine siren	105
Disco at full volume	115
Pneumatic drill nearby	120
Airplane taking off	125

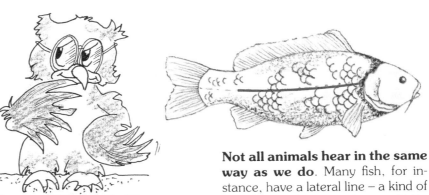

The owl cannot hear a thing with its ears. They are hidden under feather tufts on the owl's head, and are very tiny.

Not all animals hear in the same way as we do. Many fish, for instance, have a lateral line – a kind of tube filled with a special type of jelly, running down the side of the fish just under the skin. This lateral line enables the fish to pick up vibrations in the water. It can tell from the various levels of pressure of the waves whether it is a friend or a foe approaching – or something good to eat.

Crickets have their ears on their legs. These are called tympanic organs, and they work in a similar way to eardrums.

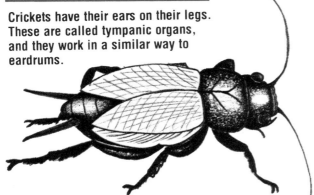

The range of sounds that a creature can make is not always the same as the range they are able to hear

Creature	Range of sounds made	Range of sounds heard
Dog	452–1080 Hz	15–50,000 Hz
Man	80–1100 Hz	20–20,000 Hz
Frog	50–8000 Hz	50–10,000 Hz
Cat	760–1520 Hz	60–65,000 Hz
Grasshopper	7000–1,000,000 Hz	100–about 28,000 Hz
Dolphin	7000–120,000 Hz	150–150,000 Hz
Robin	2000–13,000 Hz	250–21,000 Hz
Bat	10,000–120,000 Hz	1000–120,000 Hz

Do animals kiss each other?

Behavioral scientists (ethologists) try to find out why animals in a particular situation behave in one way and not in another. Living creatures have complicated behavior patterns at certain times – when they are thirsty, or want to play, or mate, for example. There are certain behavior patterns which creatures are born with, and others which are learnt after birth. Behavioral scientists are particularly interested in the question of when and how external stimuli influence the behavior of people and animals. If you observe animals and people in similar situations, it is amazing how similar their reactions are. The same ways of behaving do not always mean the same thing, however.

When two cats like each other, they sniff each other all over, push their noses together, and wash each other's coats. People who are being affectionate act in a way that is very similar. Kissing is a sign of a close relationship with someone. Scientists think that kissing is a modified form of baby or child care. You can see this kind of behavior in birds as well. The parents push food down the wide open throats of their noisy fledglings with their own beaks. It looks very similar when two adult birds are billing. Even chimpanzees 'bill' – they feed their young from mouth to mouth, and adult chimpanzees sometimes greet each other with a kiss.

People and animals are born with certain patterns of behavior – a newborn human baby automatically looks for his mother's breast, immediately grasps the nipple when he feels his mother's body, and begins to suckle. When a human baby is left alone, he cries, but he stops when someone picks him up. A baby penguin also cries if it gets lost. Its mother can distinguish her baby's voice immediately from a million other penguins. Smiling must also be inborn because human babies can smile shortly after birth.

These inborn behavioral patterns are called instincts. Reproduction· and the need for nutrition are instinctive as well. The inner need (drive) in humans and animals to reproduce is set off by chemical substances called hormones.

Usually there has to be one or more stimuli as well. For example, when the great crested grebe, a water fowl, wishes to mate, it carries out a certain inborn ritual. When the male sees a female, he starts his courtship routine and begins to woo her. He goes close to her, the birds shake their heads at each other and begin to preen their feathers. Hens behave in an odd manner sometimes. When they are hungry but have no food, they may suddenly start wildly pecking at the ground even though there is no grain there. Humans have similar reactions. If there is nothing to eat, hungry children will often suck their thumbs. Both actions are substitutes for feeding.

The threatening behavior of animals and people is often very similar. The hairs on the back of a cat's neck stand up, it spits, and bares its claws. A person pulls a frightening face, threatens with his fists.

56

There are many signals to which people and animals react. Animals have an order of precedence, just as people do, and they show higher and lower ranking by signals. For example, when two wolves meet, the dominant one holds its tail confidently up high, while the other wolf puts its tail between its legs.

You can watch these instinctive patterns in domestic pets. Cats, for example, show what they want by their actions. When a cat arches its back, it is scared. When animals want to frighten an opponent, they do their best to appear large and dangerous; a cat makes the hairs on the back of its neck stand up, its tail becomes bushy and it stretches out its claws. Its face looks menacing, too – the teeth are bared and the ears laid back. These are threatening gestures, and people use their own version of these, people threaten with their fists, breathe deeply and swell out their chests, or lean forward.

Animals mark out the boundaries of their territories very clearly with scents contained in their urine, while people build high fences and hedges round their gardens and houses. And, just like people, cats sometimes feel confused. A cat will then sit down suddenly and wash or scratch itself. People act in a similar fashion when they scratch their heads in embarrassment or confusion. Other actions indicate that you

The appearance and behavior of a small child acts as a stimulus to an adult. This is the stimulus that releases the 'baby care' routine or loving attention. Humans find chubby little people and animals appealing. Small animals and people have certain similarities. Their heads are rounded forward over their foreheads more than in adults, their faces and bodies are more rounded, with chubby cheeks, and their movements are a little awkward. Anything which is like this is seen to be 'cute' or 'sweet'. This picture shows that the same is true for animals. Now that people are aware of this, toy manufacturers all over the world make dolls and soft toys with over-large heads.

would rather run away – when you clutch the back of a chair, or grip an object tightly, for instance.

For chimpanzees, grooming is a friendly gesture. A lower-ranking chimp presents his rear to a higher-ranking one, as a sign of humility or respect. This kind of behavior avoids arguments in a group, and the weaker animals recognize the rank of the stronger. Dogs and cats lie on their backs and offer their throats to their superiors. This is only a symbolic gesture because the animal knows that the stronger one will not normally attack after such a display of humility. For people, the signs of rank are much more complicated. Differences in rank are expressed through titles, differences in income and very obviously in uniforms. People also make gestures of humility or respect, such as when they kiss someone's hand, kneel before someone or respectfully lower head or eyes. These are also called 'social' signals. For people to live happily together, it is essential that everyone understands these signals.

People have signs of respect, kneeling before a ruler or in prayer. Another sign of humility or respect is to obey everything without question. Apes avoid quarrels by the one who is inferior presenting his rear to his superior. With wolves, a higher-ranking wolf holds his tail high, while a lower-ranking one puts his tail between his legs.

When were the greatest

An invention is always something new, a new solution to a problem or a new idea. The first important invention man made was how to use fire. Fire itself is, of course, not an invention but the discovery by Stone Age Man that he could make it himself by rubbing two sticks together was epoch-making. Food could now be cooked and living quarters could be made warm. The invention of the wheel was also an important step in the history of man, just as printing, steam engines and the discovery of penicillin were. Some inventions happen more or less by accident, whereas others take craftsmen or scientists years to work out. Nowadays new discoveries are being made more and more quickly. It has been calculated that more has been invented or discovered in the last 50 years than in the thousands of years preceding them.

When was what discovered, invented, or put into use?

3800 BC: Sumerians invent the first maps

1600 BC: Phoenicians develop the alphabet

AD 851: Porcelain (China)

1040: Fireworks (China)

1317: Spectacles (Salvino Degli Amati)

1440: Book printing (Johann Gutenberg)

1510: Spring-driven clock (Peter Henlein)

1589: Water closet (Sir John Harington)

1590: Microscope (J. and Z. Janszen)

1623/4: Toothed gear calculating machine (Wilhelm Schickard)

1642: Slide rule (Edmund Gunter)

1643: Barometer (Evangelista Torricelli and V. Viviani)

1656: Pendulum clock (Christian Huygens)

1698: Steam engine (Thomas Savery)

1712: Piston steam engine (Thomas Newcomen and J. Cawley)

1765: Condenser steam engine (James Watt)

1770: India-rubber (Joseph Priestley)

1783: Hot-air balloon (Montgolfier brothers)

1792: Gas light (William Murdoch)

1797: Parachute (André-Jacques Garnerin)

1800: Battery (Alessandro Volta)

1804: Locomotive (Richard Trevithik)

1809: Glider (G. Caley)

1819: First ocean steamer voyage

1824: Portland cement (Joseph Aspdin)

1826: Photography on metal plates (J. N. Niepce) **1839** by Daguerre

1827: (Friction) matches (Walker)

1829: Steam locomotive (George Stephenson)

1829: Braille alphabet (Louis Braille)

1830: Railway Liverpool–Manchester (George Stephenson)

1831: Chloroform (Justus von Liebig)

1835: Photographs on photographic paper (W. H. Fox Talbot)

1837: Morse code (Samuel F. B. Morse)

1839/40: Bicycle (Kirkpatrick Macmillan) **1869** invention of forerunner of modern bicycle, with steering via front wheel and propulsion by rear wheel (Trefs)

1849: Safety pin

1850: Submarine (Bauer)

1854: Light bulb (Heinrich Göbel)

1858: Alarm system (Edwin T. Holmes)

1858: Sleeping car (Pullman)

1859/60: Telephone (Johann Philipp Reis)

1876: First practically applicable telephone (A. G. Bell)

1863: London Underground

1865: Sewing machine (Elias Howe)

1865/9: Laws of genetics (Mendel)

1867: Dynamite (A. Nobel)

1867: Dynamo (Werner von Siemens)

1867: Typewriter (Christopher Sholes)

1869: Margarine (Hippolyte Mege-Mouries at the request of Napoleon 3)

1872: Dining car (Pullman)

inventions?

1876: Carburettor
(Gottlieb Daimler)

1878: Light bulb
(Thomas Edison)

1877/8: Microphone
(Emil Berliner, Robert Lödgte,
David E. Hughes)

1879: Cash register
(James Ritty)

1879: Artificial sweetener (saccharin)
(Fahlberg, Remsen)

1882: First 10-storey skyscraper in
New York
(William le Baron Jersey)

1882: Electric iron
(H. W. Seeley)

1884: Fountain pen
(Lewis E. Waterman)

1885: Automobile
(Karl Benz)

1885: Motorbike
(Gottfried Daimler)

1886: Motor boat
(Gottfried Daimler)

1887: Record player
(Emil Berliner)

1888: Pneumatic bicycle tyre
(John B. Dunlop)

1889/92: Black and white film
(Thomas Edison)

1891: Zip fastener
(Whitcomb L. Judson)

1895: X-rays
(Wilhelm Conrad Röntgen)

1896 Radioactive rays
(Becquerel)

1897: Diesel motor
(Rudol Diesel)

1900: Rigid dirigible airship
(Count Ferdinand von Zeppelin)

about 1900: Gyro compass
(H. Anschütz-Kämpfe)

1901: First morse signals sent over
the Atlantic
(Guglielmo Marconi)

1902: Disc brake
(F. Lanchester)

1902: Colour photography
(Lumière company)

1903: Aeroplane with engine
(Orville and Wilbur Wright)

1907: Bakelite, first plastic material
(L. H. Baekeland)

1907: Electric washing machine
(Hurley Machine Co)

1908: Cellophane
(Dr J. Brandenburger)

1910: Principle of radio (electric arc
for music broadcasts)
(A. Seaby and C. de Forest)

1910: Neon lamp
(George Claude)

1911: Electric self-starter
(Charles Kettering)

1912: Echo (depth) sounder
(Behm)

1913: Stainless steel
(Walter Hunt)

1917: First gyroplane: forerunner of
helicopter
(Louis Bréguet)

1919: Atomic reactions
(Rutherford)

1919: Sound film
(Vogt, Massolle)

1919/20: First radio broadcasts

1922: British Broadcasting Corporation
formed

1922: Colour film
(H. Kalmus, D. F. Comstock, J.
B. Westcott)

1925/6: First mechanical television
(John Logie Baird, A. Karolus)

1927: Electronic television
(P. T. Farnsworth)

1928: Colour television
(John Logie Baird)

1928: Penicillin
(Alexander Fleming)

1930: Forerunner of stereo record

1931: Electric razor
(Jakob Schlick)

1933: Radar
(Rudolf Kühnöd)

1935: Parking meter
(Charlton C. Magee)

1937: Nylon
(Wallace H. Carothers)

1938: Ballpoint pen
(Laszlo and Georg Biro)

1939: First usable helicopter
(Igor Sikorsky)

1939: Jet aircraft
(Ernst Heinkel)

1942: V-2 rocket missile
(Weruher von Braun)

1942: Atomic reactor
(Fermi)

1942: Electronic calculating machine
(Mauchly, Eckert)

1945: Uranium atom bomb

1947: Supersonic rocket flight

1948: Transistor
(J. Bardeen, W. Shockley,
Walter Brattau)

1956: First nuclear power station

1960: Laser
(Dr Charles H. Townes)

1961: First manned space flight

1967: First heart transplant operation
(Prof Christian Barnard)

1969: First men on the moon
(Neil Armstrong and Edwin
'Buzz' Aldrin on *Apollo* II space
flight)

1971: Microprocessor
(Robert Noya, Gordon Moore)

1975: Rubik cube
(Ernö Rubik)

What has the greatest mass?

Different bodies can be compared in a variety of ways. You can compare the length, the area, the density, or the weight. To do this accurately, you need a uniform system of measurement. At one time, every country and every people had their own units of measurement. This changed at the 10th General Conference on Weights and Measures of 1954–60. For the first time, uniform descriptions and values were laid down. These are now used in nearly every country in the world.

These measurements are called SI units (short for the French 'Système International d'Unités' – international unit system). One of these systems of measurement is called mass. In simple terms, mass means roughly the same as the weight of a substance. The units are measured in kilograms (kg) and the standard unit of mass is based on that of a platinum-iridium cylinder, called the international prototype kilogram, kept at Sèvres in France.

The density or specific gravity is determined by the mass that a body displaces in a certain volume. The measurement for this is kg/m³. A body is said to have a density of 1 kg/m³ if it weighs 1 kilogram and takes up the space of 1 m³.

Sometimes the density is also given as the specific gravity, as with different types of wood, for example. Woods with a specific gravity below 0.55 are particularly soft and those with a specific gravity above this are harder.

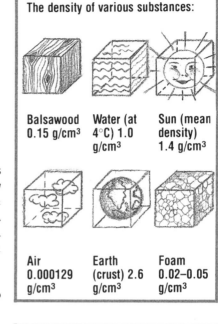

The density of various substances:

| Balsawood 0.15 g/cm³ | Water (at 4°C) 1.0 g/cm³ | Sun (mean density) 1.4 g/cm³ |
| Air 0.000129 g/cm³ | Earth (crust) 2.6 g/cm³ | Foam 0.02–0.05 g/cm³ |

Soft		Hard	
Balsa	0.15	Walnut	0.61
Fir	0.41	Birch	0.63
Spruce	0.43	Hazelnut	0.63
Willow	0.46	Teak	0.65
Chestnut	0.53	Plum	0.69
Cherry	0.55	Rosewood	0.95
Larch	0.55	Ebony	1.25

Diamond

Sapphire

Ruby

Emerald

Precious stones are measured in carats. Carats are the dried seeds of the St John's bread tree. Carats were once used in Africa to weigh out gold, and in India to weigh diamonds. Nowadays the metric carat has become a standard measurement which is used in most countries. 1 carat = 200 milligram = 0.2 gram.

Before it became a standard measurement, the term 'carat' meant all sorts of different weights in different countries. An Austrian carat, for example, was 206.1 milligram, and an English carat was 205.3 milligram. Gold is treated rather differently. The carat value indicates the purity of the gold rather than the weight. 24 carat gold is pure gold, whilst 8 carat gold contains only a third gold with the remainder made up of other metals.

A fully-grown elephant has a mass of 4000 kg or 4 tonnes.

60

Mass

The mass of the universe or the sun is so great that you cannot write all the figures one after another. So a special method of writing these masses is used.

Some masses to compare

Universe	about 10^{50} kg
Milky Way	4.4×10^{41} kg
Sun	1.993×10^{30} kg
Earth	5.997×10^{24} kg
Moon	7.35×10^{22} kg
Waters of the oceans	1.4×10^{21} kg
Blue whale	over 100,000 kg
Locomotive	100,000 kg
Elephant	4000 kg
Rhinoceros	2500 kg
Average family car	1000 kg
Wild boar	200 kg
Lion	130 kg
Adult man	about 75 kg
12 year-old child	about 35 kg
Sparrow	6×10^{-3} kg = 0.006 g

Viruses are so tiny that some cannot be seen even with a microscope. The ratio of the mass of a virus to the mass of a person is like the ratio of that person to the mass of the earth. Can you imagine that?

Approximate conversion table

1 kilogram
　(kg) = 1000 gram (g)
1 gram
　(g) = 1000 milligram (mg)
1 tonne
　(t) = 1000 kilogram (kg)
1 pound
　(lb) = 0.5 kg = 500 g
1 hundredweight
　(cwt) = 50 kg

A 12-year-old has an average mass of 35 kg. 114 children would have the same mass as an elephant.

Only about half that number of children are shown here, 114 of them would have taken up the whole page!

61

According to the latest figures from America, there are roughly 5 billion people living on the earth. Twenty-one per cent of these live in North America, Europe, and the Soviet Union (the industrial countries). More than two-thirds of the people live in the poor countries of the world (the developing countries). According to the American scientists' calculations, there will be 6.2 billion people on earth in the year 2000, more than half of them in towns which will be constantly increasing in size. China, Nigeria and India will then have the largest populations.

Not everyone can read and write, and those who cannot are known as analphabetical or illiterate. There are more illiterate women than there are men, because attending school is forbidden to women in many countries of the world. Nowadays, one in four people cannot read and write, but 35 years ago it was almost one in two people. In every country in the world, great efforts are being made to help everyone to read and write.

If the whole world contained only 100 children, there would be:
58 Asian children
11 African children
9 South American children
6 Soviet children
6 North American children
9 European children
and 1 child from the whole of the rest of the world.

How many people *cannot* read and write? (as a percentage of the population)	
	per cent
Great Britain	3.6
Germany	1
Italy	4.4
Greece	14
Whole of Europe and USSR	5
North America	about 10
South America	27
Nigeria	66
Kenya	52
Algeria	55
Whole of Africa	75
Afghanistan	80
People's Republic of China	34.5
Turkey	31.2
India (unreliable statistics)	34
Whole of Asia	50

In Africa, three out of four children cannot read or write; in Asia, two out of four, and in South America, one out of four.

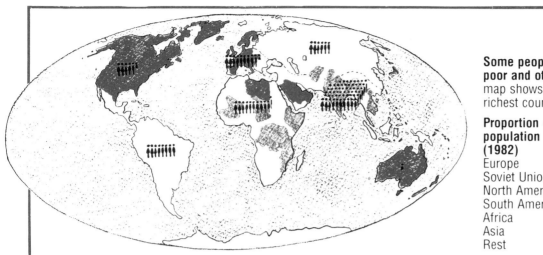

Some people in the world are poor and others are rich. This map shows the poorest and the richest countries of the world.

Proportion of the world's population as a percentage (1982)

Europe	9.4
Soviet Union	5.9
North America	5.6
South America	8.2
Africa	10.9
Asia	58.3
Rest	1.7

The population of the world is increasing very rapidly. This table shows how many people there have been on earth in the years 1900–1980, and how many there are likely to be in the year 2025.

Development of population (in millions)

	1900	1950	1980	2000	2025
Whole world	1650	2486	4432	6200	8195
Europe (without USSR)	296	392	484	512	522
America	156	328	612	865	1208
North America	82	166	248	299	343
South America	74	162	364	566	865
Africa	133	217	470	853	1542
Asia	925	1355	2579	3550	4531
Eastern Asia		669	1175	1475	1712
Southern Asia		686	1404	2075	2819
USSR	134	180	265	310	355

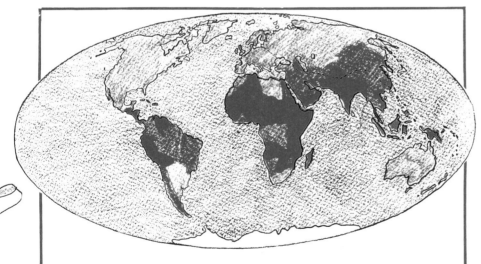

On a world-wide scale, every woman between the ages of 15 and 45 has, on average, 3.5 children. (Of course that does *not* mean that some women have only half a baby! This is the average figure for the number of births per woman.) In some parts of the world women have considerably more children than women in other parts. Even in one country, there is often a great difference between the number of children women have.

Many people are starving, or cannot get enough nourishment to stay healthy. In other parts of the world, people have too much food. Sometimes they eat so much that they become ill. This drawing shows where people have too much food, where they have enough food, and where they are starving.

Too much food
1.7 million

Enough food
1.8 million

Starving
1.5 million

How many children do women have in:

Europe	1.9
Asia	3.5
China	2.3
Japan	1.7
India	4.6
South America	4.1
North America	1.8
Africa	6.4

Who has what?

Many of the people in the developing countries of the world are farmers, and most of them just grow enough food to live on. In the richer countries, also known as the industrial countries, some people work the land, but more work in factories of some kind. A few countries, such as the Arab states, are wealthy because they possess rich resources of valuable oil. The four richest countries of the world – the USA, the Soviet Union, Japan and Germany – possess 50 per cent of the world's wealth, and yet account for only 21 per cent of the world's population.

The wealth of a country is measured not only by the average income of its people, but also by the so-called standard of living. This refers to how people live and what their houses are like, whether they have running water and electricity in their homes, and whether there are services such as medical facilities available to them if they need them. Rich countries have a high standard of living, whereas in poor countries there are many homes without water or electricity.

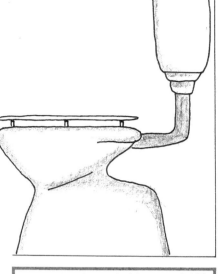

How many lorries are there per 1000 people?	
Great Britain	11
Germany	25
Denmark	53
Luxembourg	28
Sweden	21
Spain	32
Greece	33
Yugoslavia	12
Algeria	10
Kenya	10
Argentina	47
Brazil	8
Canada	104
USA	136
India	less than 1
Japan	110
Australia	98

How many households out of 100 have a toilet?	
Great Britain	97
Australia	98
Germany	96
Hungary	94
Brazil	53
Algeria	34
Sri Lanka	9

How many private cars are there per 1000 people?	
Great Britain	351
Germany	353
Denmark	289
Luxembourg	362
Sweden	345
Spain	176
Greece	80
Yugoslavia	48
Algeria	8
Kenya	6
Argentina	109
Brazil	67
Canada	408
USA	524
India	1
Japan	185
Australia	398

The number of patients per doctor in some Third World Countries:	
India	4162 patients
Chad (Africa)	44,382 patients
Guatemala	3641 patients
Malawi	76,589 patients
Colombia	2106 patients
Thailand	7531 patients

How many people out of 100 have a telephone?	
Great Britain	40
Germany	48
Denmark	61
Luxembourg	50
Sweden	77
Spain	30
Greece	28
Yugoslavia	1569 people share a telephone
Algeria	2
Kenya	1
Argentina	10
Canada	65
USA	81
India	261 people share a telephone
Japan	47
Australia	50

How many people are there per radio?

Great Britain	1
Germany	1
Denmark	1
Luxembourg	2
Sweden	1
Spain	4
Greece	3.4
Yugoslavia	4.8
Algeria	6.3
Kenya	29
Argentina	2.8
Brazil	7.2
Canada	1 person possesses almost 2 radios
USA	1 person possesses 2 radios
India	33
Japan	1.8
Australia	1

How many households out of 100 have electricity?

Great Britain	99
Germany	98
Denmark	96
Canada	94
Brazil	53

How many households out of 100 have running water?

Great Britain	99
Germany	99
Denmark	98
Canada	96
USA	96
Brazil	33
Tunisia	14
Sri Lanka	4

How many people are there per television set?

Great Britain	2
Germany	2
Denmark	2
Luxembourg	4
Sweden	2.7
Spain	5
Greece	8
Yugoslavia	5.3
Algeria	34
Kenya	255
Argentina	6
Brazil	11
Canada	2
USA	1.6
India	850
Japan	1.9
Australia	2.9

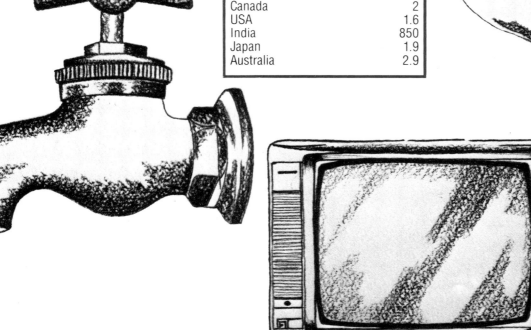

How much can a child carry?

Why do people keep firmly on the ground? The pulling power working from the center of the earth is called gravity. This power is so great that we always stand firmly on our two legs and objects always fall downwards. The fact is that the gravity of an object like the earth is determined by its mass: the greater the mass and the closer it is to another object, the greater the gravity. For example, the further a spaceship flies from the earth, the less effect the power of gravity has on the spaceship and the lighter it becomes. At a distance of 6400 km/4000 miles from the earth it weighs only a quarter of its original weight. At 38,000 km/24,000 miles it weighs only about 2 per cent of its original weight.

When a spaceship comes close to the moon it is affected by the moon's gravity. This is much lower than that of the earth, however, because the moon has much less mass than the earth – only about 17 per cent or about a sixth. The gravity of the moon is therefore only about a sixth of the earth's gravity. That is why an astronaut on the moon can jump six times higher and can carry loads six times heavier than he can on the earth.

A child, if he tries really hard, can carry three or four shopping bags (30 kg/66 lb) at the same time. With the same effort on the moon he could carry at least 180 kg/400 lb. That is the equivalent of about 18 shopping bags or the weight of five 12-year-old children.

Of course, it is not only the earth and the moon that have powers of gravity. The gravity of other planets can also be measured. If we say the gravity of the earth is 1, the gravity of the other planets is:

Gravity	
Sun	27.88
Mercury	0.3771
Venus	0.9034
Mars	0.3795
Jupiter	2.644
Saturn	1.139
Uranus	0.912
Neptune	1.2
Pluto	0.04

Gravity

A child jumping 1 meter/3 feet high on earth could jump only 3.6 cm/1¼ inches on the sun because its gravity is far higher. On Jupiter he could reach 38 cm/15 inches, on Neptune 83 cm/28 inches and on Saturn 8 cm/30 inches. Only on Uranus, which has a lower gravity than the earth, could the child, using the same effort as on earth, jump higher than 1 meter/3 feet – 1.10 meters/3 feet 6 inches to be exact. On Venus it would be just 1 centimeter more, 1.11 meters/3 feet 6½ inches. On Mars he could easily manage the 2.63 meter/8 feet 7 inches mark, on Mercury it would be 2.65 meters/8 feet 8 inches and on Pluto 25 meters/83 feet.

The gravity at any point on the earth has the same effect on different weights. That is why two stones of different weights thrown out of a high-rise building would reach the ground at the same time – but only if they were of the same shape. The same would be true, in principle, of a stone and a feather. But a feather has a completely different shape from a stone, and therefore has a different resistance to the air, so it would reach the ground later than the stone. The reason is not its lower weight but that its shape makes it float to the ground.

The tides of the sea also rely on gravity of the moon and the sun. The moon's gravity is more noticeable than that of the sun because the moon is closer to the earth. The gravity of the moon pulls in the water masses of the oceans. The result is a kind of water mountain which

Using the same amount of effort, children could jump much higher on the moon than on the earth. That is because the moon has a lower power of gravity than the earth – only about a sixth. This astronaut could take a run and jump over five of his friends, and he could carry loads six times as heavy as he could on earth.

The moon and the sun pull up the water masses of the earth. The result is water mountains (high tide) which follow the moon on its journey around the earth. Between the water mountains lie the low tide zones. (above)
The tides are especially high during a full moon, when the sun and the moon pull the water up together.

follows the moon as it circles the earth. The water mountain is pulled in towards the shore, and we get high tide. Then it is pulled away, and we get low tide. The gravity of the sun also produces a water mountain but it is much smaller than that of the moon. Very high and very low tides ('spring tides') occur during a full and a new moon. Then the sun, moon and earth form a line and the pull of gravity on the water masses of the earth is especially high. During the first and fourth moon quarter, the sun, moon and earth form a right angle. This means the gravities are reduced and the difference between low and high tide is especially low ('neap tide').

How many noughts in 10^{12}?

Our ancestors used pebbles, sticks, parts of their body or knots for counting. This system has its drawbacks, though. You soon get far too many pebbles and sticks. The decimal system we use today was made possible by the Indians when they invented the nought. Today the decimal system of counting has been adopted internationally and is used in most countries in the world, though some countries use the numerical system of their ancestors as well.

The way we write our numbers comes from the Arabs. With small numbers our system is quite satisfactory. The first digit shows the ones, the second the tens, the third the hundreds and the fourth the thousands. But we get into difficulties when we reach the million mark because we need to count how many digits we have. Who knows the name of a 1 with 12 noughts? To save counting, powers or potencies have been introduced. Instead of writing 1 with 12 noughts, you write 10^{12}.

If you want to show 5,000,000,000,000 you write 5.10^{12}; 80,000 is written 8.10^4, and so on. It is also difficult to show numbers which are smaller than 1. For this we use negative potencies.

0.1	one tenth	10^{-1}
0.01	one hundredth	10^{-2}
0.001	one thousandth	10^{-3}
0.0001	one ten thousandth	10^{-4}
0.00001	one hundred thousandth	10^{-5}
0.000001	one millionth	10^{-6}

England and America use different names for some numbers, so beware:

US

1 billion	$= 10^9$	= 1 milliard
1 trillion	$= 10^{12}$	= 1 billion
1 quadrillion	$= 10^{15}$	= 1 billiard
1 quintillion	$= 10^{18}$	= 1 trillion
1 sextillion	$= 10^{21}$	= 1 trilliard
1 septillion	$= 10^{24}$	= 1 quadrillion
1 octillion	$= 10^{27}$	= 1 quadrillard
1 nonillion	$= 10^{30}$	= 1 quadrillard

Numbers can also be expressed using the binary system. The decimal system has a base 10, using symbols 1 to 9. The binary system has a base 2, using only the symbols 1 and 0. It is the basic number language of computers because, although it is cumbersome for us to use, computers work so quickly that this does not matter. Also, the electric current can react to these two symbols. 0 and 1 correspond to a switch off and on. In the binary system $1 = 0 + 1$; $2 = 1 + 1 = 10$; $3 = 1 + 1 + 1 = 11$; $4 = 10 + 10 = 100$, and so on. The numbers 1–25 are expressed as follows:

Decimal	Binary	Decimal	Binary
0	0	13	1101
1	1	14	1110
2	10	15	1111
3	11	16	10000
4	100	17	10001
5	101	18	10010
6	110	19	10011
7	111	20	10100
8	1000	21	10101
9	1001	22	10110
10	1010	23	10111
11	1011	24	11000
12	1100	25	11001

Numbers and Potencies

1	one	10^0
10	ten	10^1
100	(one) hundred	10^2
1 000	(one) thousand	10^3
10 000	ten thousand	10^4
100 000	(one) hundred thousand	10^5
1 000 000	one million	10^6
10 000 000	ten million	10^7
100 000 000	(one) hundred million	10^8
1 000 000 000	(one) milliard	10^9
10 000 000 000	ten milliard	10^{10}
100 000 000 000	(one) hundred milliard	10^{11}
1 000 000 000 000	one billion	10^{12}
10 000 000 000 000	ten billion	10^{13}
100 000 000 000 000	(one) hundred billion	10^{14}
1 000 000 000 000 000	one billiard	10^{15}
10 000 000 000 000 000	ten billiard	10^{16}
100 000 000 000 000 000	(one) hundred billiard	10^{17}
1 000 000 000 000 000 000	one trillion	10^{18}
(one) thousand trillion	one trilliard	10^{21}
1 million trillion	one quadrillion	10^{24}
1 million quadrillion	one quintillion	10^{30}
1 million quintillion	one sextillion	10^{36}
1 million sextillion	one septillion	10^{42}
1 million septillion	one octillion	10^{48}
1 million octillion	one nonillion	10^{54}
10 000 septillion nonillion	one googol	10^{100}

Counting Systems

Writing out the figures isn't the only way to show numbers. They can also be arranged in other ways. Pascal's triangle is one example. It evolves from adding up the two upper numbers like this:

```
                    1
                 1     1
              1     2     1
           1     3     3     1
        1     4     6     4     1
     1     5    10    10     5     1
   1     6    16    20    15     6     1
 1     7    21    35    35    21     7     1
1    8    28    56    70    56    28     8     1
1   9   36   84  126  126   84   36    9     1
1  10  45  120 210 252 210 120   45   10    1
```

The sum of the figures in the rows of the triangle are the potencies of 2:

$1 = 2^0$	$64 = 2^6$
$2 = 2^1$	$128 = 2^7$
$4 = 2^2$	$256 = 2^8$
$8 = 2^3$	$512 = 2^9$
$16 = 2^4$	$1024 = 2^{10}$
$32 = 2^5$	

Looking at Pascal's triangle it is easy to see how the potencies of two are built up.

It is useful when calculating statistics, probability calculus and insurance.

Another way of expressing numbers is the pyramid: A pyramid has four corners and a point. The smallest pyramid is made up of five spheres: one at each corner and one at the top. The next pyramid has 14 spheres, nine on the first level, four on the next and one at the top. It is worked out like this: Small pyramid: $1 + 2^2 = 1 + 4 = 15$

the next pyramid is: $1 + 2^2 + 3^2 = 1 + 4 + 9 = 15$

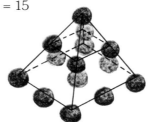

The pyramid this child is building should have $1 + 2^2 + 3^2 + 4^2 + 5^2 + 6^2 + 7^2$ balls. Have fun working it out!

Solution: The pyramid is made of 140 balls altogether (1 + 4 + 9 + 16 + 25 + 36 + 49)

1980

The year 1980 written in eight different ways:

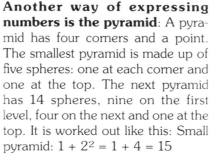

This is how the **Babylonians** wrote their numbers.

The numbering system of the **Egyptians** was based on the number 10. Numbers 1 to 9 were written as strokes, one stroke per number. Numbers 10 to 90 were shown as hooks; for example, eight hooks for 80. The snails show the hundreds (nine snails for 900). The half-moon on the stand shows 1000.

The ancient **Hebrews** used letters as numbers.

The ancient **Greeks** also used letters for numbers. This was the Ionic numbering system.

MCMLXXX

The numbering system of the **Romans** is still in use today. I is 1, V is 5, X is 10, L is 50, C is 100, D is 500, M is 1000. If there are three III together, that means it is 3, three VVV is 15. Only three of the same symbol can be used in one number. You can't write XXXX for 40, for example. It becomes XL, that means it is really 50 − 10. 4 is not written IIII but IV (5 − 1). 90 isn't LXXXX but LXL or XC (50 + 40 or 100 − 10).

The **Hindu** numbering system has a specific meaning, similar to our numbering system today. It was the ancient **Indians** who 'discovered' the figure 0.

1980 in **Chinese**

The ancient **Arabs and Hindus** used similar numbering systems. We adopted our method of writing numbers from the Arabs and developed it further.

What has the best eyesight?

The human eye can project images to the brain like a camera. Not all creatures have eyes which can do that. The eye's capacity to see depends on the way it is constructed. The eye in its simplest form is a light sensitive skin cell found in moluscs and earthworms. The eye of human beings and vertebrate animals is a highly developed lens. Like a camera, it is optically equipped to recognize shapes and images. The incoming light is concentrated and projected on to the back of the eyeball, the retina. Here there are millions of visual rod and cone cells. The rods differentiate between light and dark and the cones distinguish color.

The lens-type eye is the most highly developed light sensory organ. The edible snail has eyes of similar construction, but it cannot see images. This is due to the lack of sufficient visual cells on the retina. The more visual cells there are in the eye, the better the brain can recognize fine detail. The peregrine falcon has about 1.3 million visual cells per square millimeter, human beings have only 160,000 per square millimeter. The falcon can see a mouse from a distance of 1500 meters/4572 feet. At the same distance the human eye can only recognize an animal if it is at least the size of a deer. The eye is equipped with additional features which improve its ability to see clearly. There are muscles which alter the curvature of the lens so that we can see objects clearly from close up and from far away. The pupils regulate the light intake, and muscles outside the eye are necessary to judge distances correctly.

Even more fascinating are the compound or facet eyes of many insects. They consist of a number of separate hexagonal eyes with usually eight visual cells. The overall picture is made up of many separate images, like a mosaic. The more separate eyes the insect has, the more sharply it can see. The earwig has only five of these facets, a worker ant has 600, a bumble bee about 4000, the may beetle has over 5470 and a dragonfly has 10,000 facet eyes, enabling it to pounce on prey at a flying speed of 50 kph/30 mph. An ant, with just 600 facets, only notices an obstacle when it has almost run into it.

What are optical deceptions?

The eyes can estimate a distance but a separate eye movement is necessary for each distance. The movements are controlled by the sensory muscle within the eye muscles. As we are not all born with an accurate eye, our eyes can be deceived – optical deception. Horizontal lines seem shorter than vertical lines. The reason is that horizontal eye movements are less strenuous than vertical ones. If the eye is led upwards or downwards by lines, the image appears larger or smaller. And an object always seems smaller in large surroundings than in small surroundings.

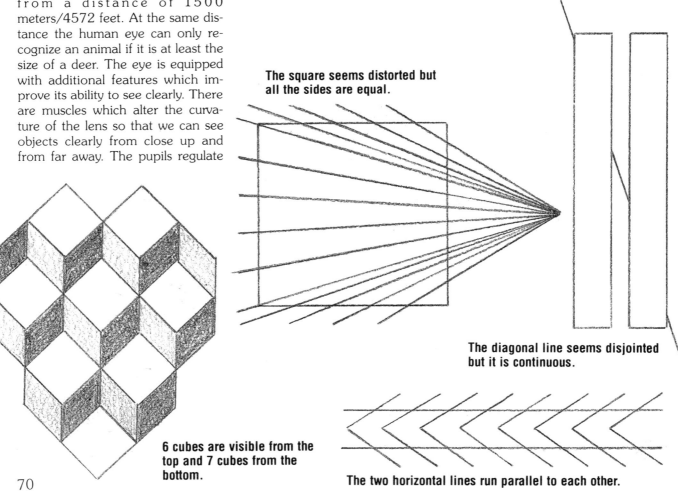

The square seems distorted but all the sides are equal.

6 cubes are visible from the top and 7 cubes from the bottom.

The diagonal line seems disjointed but it is continuous.

The two horizontal lines run parallel to each other.

Bees cannot see as many colors as humans. They can only differentiate between three color groups: yellow (orange, yellow, green), blue-green and blue (blue, purple). Bees can see short-wave ultraviolet light which is invisible to the human eye. Human beings can differentiate between 250 pure colors, 17,000 mixed colors and 300 shades of gray (white to black), about 10 million colors in all. In addition, the human eye has three to six million cones to see color and around 100 million rods to see light and dark. The color sensitivity of the budgerigar is surprising because it is almost as good as that of people. The eyes of nocturnal birds and animals like the owl have mainly rods, which makes them more or less color-blind. The nocturnal animals include the house mouse, house rat, golden hamster and coyote. The eyes of diurnal creatures (those that hunt by day) have mainly cones.

Which animal can see which colors?

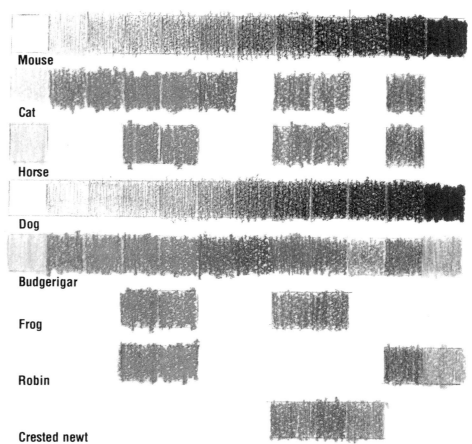

Mouse

Cat

Horse

Dog

Budgerigar

Frog

Robin

Crested newt

The vertical line is the same length as the horizontal line.

The distance from a–b is the same length as the distance from b–c.

Why do cats' eyes glow in the dark? Cats, like many other predators, belong to the group of nocturnal animals. There is an area behind the retina which reflects light. The reason that nocturnal animals can see better at dusk is that the reflection activates the visual cells twice, causing the eyes to glow.

Facet eyes, as found in bees and other insects cannot break up an image into details as well as the lens-type eyes of humans. If two dots are only 1 millimeter apart, the human eye can still see them even from a distance of several meters/feet. The bee cannot see the dots if it is more than 7.5 cm/3 inches away from them.

How big is a foot?

It seems amazing that around 200 years ago nearly every country in the world had its own measuring system. People then did not have the metric system almost universally used today. Our ancestors used measures that related either to their bodies (e.g. foot, ell, or span) or to what they could accomplish (a 'morning' or a 'stone's throw').

Not only was this way of measuring very inaccurate, but it also varied from city to city, country to country, continent to continent. A foot in Prussia measured between 31.4 and 37.6 cm/12½ and 15 inches. In Italy it was 30.48 cm/12 inches and the foot of a trader from elsewhere was less than 28 cm/11 inches long. The measuring of longer distances must have been quite funny to watch. To work out the width of a road in the 16th century 16 men had to stand very close behind each other. Some of these measuring units are used today, but now they are accurately defined: a foot, for example, is now exactly 30.48 cm/12 inches long, and a yard exactly 91.44 cm/36 inches.

All the confusion changed with the French Revolution. A meter was supposed to be a meter wherever you were. The prototype meter was established in Paris. This was the equivalent of a 10 millionth part of a quarter of the earth (the shortest distance between equator and pole). But the prototype meter itself already deviates, fractionally, from the established norm. Since 1960 we have a new definition for the meter: by measuring the light radiation of the chemical element krypton, available in a vacuum in a specific form, the meter is calculated as 1,650,763.73 times the wavelength of the orange line of the krypton iso-tope. Not all countries in the world are satisfied with that measuring unit alone: in Britain imperial measures are used as well as metric, and in the USA only the imperial measures are in general use.

The 'morning' was an agricultural measuring unit. It meant what you might imagine it to mean. It was the size of a piece of land which a farmer could work with a horse-drawn plough in one morning. As you can imagine, it was not a very accurate system!

There are some other old measures which used parts of the body as a guide, in the same way that the foot does. The span was the length of the hand span, from tip of the thumb to the little finger with the fingers spread. A cubit was the distance between finger tips and elbow. Horses are measured in hands. Today this is a standard 10 cm/4 inches which is about the width of an adult hand.

It wasn't easy for traders of previous centuries when they wanted to work out exactly how many ells they could cut from a piece of material. In France an ell measured 139 cm/55 inches, in England 115 cm/45 inches, and in Flanders, part of modern Belgium, an ell was only 65 cm/26 inches long.

Measurements

Children's clothing sizes

British and Continental Height (cm)	American Age	Chest size (inches)	X-sizes
116	6		
122	7		
128	8		
134	9		
140	10		
146	11		
152	12		
158	13	26	XS
164	14	27	S
170	15	28	M
176	16	30	L
182	17	31	XL
188	18	32	XL

It's not easy to find the right size if there are four different sizing systems for children's clothes to choose from.

The measuring system of Old England

1 inch	= 1/12 ft = 0.02615 m
1 foot	= 12 in = 1/12 pole = 0.3138 m
1 ell	= 45 in = 1.143 m
1 fathom	= 72 in = 6 ft = 2½ poles = 1.883 m
1 pole	= 198 in = 16 ft = 5.0292 m
1 mile	= 5280 ft = 1760 yds = 1609.3 m

The measuring system of Ancient Greece

1 stadion	= 6 plethra	= 184.98 m/202.3 yds
1 plethron	= 100 ft	= 30.83 m/33.75 yds
1 orgyia (fathom)	= 6 ft	= 1.85 m/2.01 yds
1 pechys (ell)	= 1 ft	= 0.462 m/18 in
1 pus (foot)	= 16 daktyloi	= 0.3083 m/12 in
1 palaiste (hand)	= 4 daktyloi	= 0.0771 m/3 in
1 daktylos (finger)		= 0.0193 m/0.75 in

The measuring system of Ancient Rome

1 milliarium (mile)	= 1000 passus	= 1478.71 m/1611.78 yds
1 passus (pace or double step)	= 5 pedes	= 1.48 m/5 ft
1 pes (foot)	= 4 palmi	= 0.296 m/12 in
1 palmus (hand)		= 0.074 m/3 in
1 cubitus (ell)	= 24 digiti = 1.5 pedes	= 0.444 m/17 in
1 digitus (finger)		= 0.0185 m/0.07 in

Linear measures used in most countries today

1 meter (m)	= 10 decimeters (dm)
	= 100 centimeters (cm)
	= 1000 millimeters (mm)
1 kilometer (km)	= 1000 meters

Imperial linear measures

1 inch (in)	2.54 cm
1 foot (ft) = 12 in	30.48 cm
1 yard (yd) = 3 ft	91.44 cm
1 pole = 5 yd	5.03 m
1 chain = 4 poles	20.12 m
1 furlong = 10 chains	201.17m
1 mile = 8 furlongs	1.603 km

Sailors use their own measures

1 fathom = 6 ft	1.829 m
1 cable length = 100 fathoms	182.9 m
1 nautical mile	1852 m
1 knot = 1 nautical mile per hour	

There are also two different systems for measuring area

1 square meter (m²)	= 100 dm²
	= 10,000 cm²
	= 1,000,000 mm²
1 are (a) = 100 m²	
1 hectare (ha) = 100 a	
1 square kilometer (km²) = 100 ha	

1 square inch (sq in)	6.45 cm²
1 sq ft = 144 sq in	9.28 dm²
1 sq yd = 9 sq ft	0.836 m²
1 rod, pole, perch = 30 sq yd	25.289 m²
1 rood = 40 rod	10.12 a
1 acre = 4 rood	0.4048 ha
1 sq mile	2.59 km²

Finding the right shoes isn't always easy. There are three sizing systems for shoes, the British, the Continental and the American. Use this table to guide you.

American	4	4½	5	5½	6	6½	7	7½	8	8½
British	2	3	3½	4	4½	5	5½	6	6½	7
Continental	35	35½	36	36½	37	37½	38	38½	39	40
American	9	9½	10	10½	11	11½	12	12½	13	13½
British	7½	8	8½	9	9½	10	10½	11	11½	12
Continental	41	42	42½	43	44	44½	45	46	46½	47

Highest mountains and

The highest mountain in Britain is Ben Nevis, which is 1343 meters/ 4406 feet high, not counting the cairn which gives it an extra 3.65 meters/12 feet. The highest peak in North America is Mount McKinley at 6194 meters/20,440 feet.

The famous German naturalist, Alexander von Humboldt (1769–1859), wanted to climb the highest mountains and discover the deepest depths of the oceans. In 1802 Humboldt climbed the volcano Chimborazo in Equador, which is 6265 meters/20,561 feet high. Although he had to abandon the climb at a height of 5760 meters/19,000 feet, he held the world mountain-climbing record for nearly 30 years. But it was not until after his death that the deepest areas of the oceans could be explored with the aid of modern diving equipment, diving bells (bathyspheres) and diving ships (bathyscaphes). Among the most famous deep-sea explorers were Auguste Piccard and his son Jacques. In 1953, Auguste reached a depth of 3150 meters/10,330 feet, using a diving ship with diving bells attached. Jacques later reached the deepest point of the oceans, the Marianas Trench (11,000 meters/36,300 feet) from the diving ship *Trieste*.

What lives at the bottom of the sea? At a depth of 400 meters/1320 feet the water is almost motionless and because hardly any light reaches that depth, no plants can exist. Deep-sea fish feed on dead plankton (minute animals and plants floating in the water) or they are predators and eat their own species. Deep-sea fish have adapted to their dark surroundings: some are blind but are equipped with long, delicate antennae, sensitive legs or barbels with which they can feel things. Other inhabitants of the deep-sea have highly sensitive telescopic eyes or luminous organs like a torch above their heads.

Deep-sea trenches are narrow channels at the bottom of oceans more than 5500 meters/18,000 feet deep. There are 22 deep-sea trenches in the Pacific Ocean, three in the Atlantic and one in the Indian Ocean. Calculating the depth is often inaccurate as nobody can measure out the deep-sea trenches by hand. When echo-sounding the depths, the density of the water, the temperature and the salt content all have to be taken into account. In the Marianas Trench, for example, depths between 10,900 and 11,034 meters/36,000 and 36,500 feet below sea level have been calculated.

Using diving bells (bathyspheres), explorers were able to reach depths of 923 m/3046 feet and even 1268 m/4184 feet in 1934.

The depths some deep-sea submarines have reached	m/ft
Archimedes (1961)	11,000/36,300
Trieste II (1964)	11,000/36,300
Alvin (1965)	3600/11,880
Aluminaut (1965)	5000/16,500
Deepstar 400 (1966)	130/5300

deepest depths

Mountains and valleys

The highest mountain is Mount Everest at 8848 meters/29,000 feet above sea level. Situated in the Himalayas, it is called Chu-mu-lang-ma by the Chinese, Mi-ti Gu-ti Cha-pu Long-na by the Tibetans and Sagarmatha by the Nepalese. Since 1921 several mountaineers have tried to conquer Mount Everest and 11 lives have been lost in the attempt. It was not until 29 May 1953 that the New Zealander Edmund P. Hillary and his Sherpa, Tensing Norgay, finally succeeded in reaching the summit. The Himalayas, together with the Karakoram, Hindukush and Pamir is the world's tallest mountain range with 92 peaks of over 7500 meters/25,000 feet. The second highest mountain range is the Andes in South America with 54 peaks of over 6100 meters/20,130 feet.

The highest mountain of each continent		
Mount Everest	Nepal (Asia)	8848 m/29,000 ft
Mount Aconcagua	Argentina (South America)	6960 m/23,000 ft
Mount McKinley	Alaska (North America)	6194 m/20,440 ft
Kilimanjaro	Tanzania (Africa)	5894 m/19,450 ft
Elbrus (Western summit)	USSR (Eastern Europe)	5633 m/18,588 t
Vinson Massif	Antarctica	5140 m/16,864 ft
Jayakusumu	Oceania	4883 m/16,113 ft
Mont Blanc	France (Western Europe)	4807 m/15,863 ft

How deep are the oceans?

	average depth	deepest point
Atlantic Ocean	3332 m/10,995 ft	9219 m/30,422 ft
Indian Ocean	3840 m/12,672 ft	7455 m/24,601 ft
Pacific Ocean	4028 m/13,292 ft	11,033 m/36,408 ft
Mediterranean	1430 m/4,719 ft	5267 m/17,381 ft
North Sea	93 m/307 ft	729 m/2,405 ft
Baltic	55 m/181 ft	459 m/1,514 ft

Although 'only' 4205 meters/13,876 feet of Mauna Kea, on Hawaii Island, ('white mountain') are visible above sea level it is actually the highest mountain on earth, because 5998 meters/19,793 feet of it are hidden below the sea! Measured from the foot, it has an astonishing height of 10,203 meters/33,670 feet.

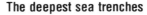

The deepest sea trenches

Length km/miles	Area	Deepest point	Depth m/ft
2250/1395	Marianas Trench (West Pacific)	Challenger or Witjas Depth I	11,033–10,900/ 36,408–35,970
2575/1596	Tonga Trench	Witjas Depth II	10,882/35,910
1325/821	Philippine Trench	Galathea Depth	10,540/34,782
6500/4030	Bonin Trench (West Pacific) (with 4 other trenches)	Ramapo Depth	10,340/34,122
2300/1426	Kermadec Trench (South Pacific)	Witjas Depth III	10,047/33,155
3000/1860	Puerto-Rico Trench (Atlantic)	Milwaukee Depth	9219/30,422

How fast can a snail travel?

When calculating these speeds, it is assumed that man, animal or machine move in the same way. The distance traveled and the time taken form the basis of the calculation. The distance is measured in meters/feet and the time in seconds. If an object needs 1 second to travel 1 meter or foot it has a speed of 1 m/s or 1 ft/s.

Speed can be expressed in different measuring units for time and distance. Very fast objects are calculated in kilometers or miles per second or even as the speed of light.

Very slow objects are measured in millimeters per day or month. A fingernail for example grows at a speed of 7 millimeters per month.

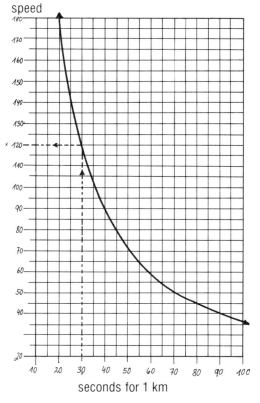

seconds for 1 km

Metric conversion table

Speed of light: 300,000 km/s

Light year: The distance the light travels during one year = 9.463 billion km or 5.867 billion miles

1 m/s = 3.6 km/h = 60 m/min = 100 cm/s

1 km/h = 0.2778 m/s = 16.667 m/m = 1 kilometer per hour

Mach = for speeds that are faster than the speed of sound = M

M 1 = speed of sound = 340 m/s = about 1200 km/h = 744 mph

M 2 = 680 m/s = about 2400 km/h = 1488 mph

M 0.5 = 170 m/s = about 600 km/h = 372 mph

Knots = kn = the sailing speed of a ship

1 kn = 1 nautical mile per hour = 1.852 km/h = 1.148 mph

Imperial conversion table

1 mile per hour = 1 mph = 1.6093 km/h

1 km/h = 0.6214 mph

1 yard per minute = 1 yd/min = 0.9144 m/min = 1.524 cm/s

1 foot per second = 1 ft/s = 0.3048 m/s = 18.82 m/min

1 inch per second = 1 in/s = 2.54 cm/s = 0.0254 m/s

1 British knot = 1 UKkn = 1.8531 km/h = 1.000592 kn

You can calculate different speeds using this graph and a stop watch or watch with a second hand. For example, it takes a car 50 seconds to travel 1 kilometer. To find the car's speed, look along the bottom line until you reach 50. Now trace a line up from 50 until you reach the speed curve. Draw a horizontal line from this point on the curve to the speed line on the left. You will see that the car is traveling at 70 kph.

The fastest snail: 0.0138 meters/s 0.414 feet/s   **Walking is 100 times faster**   **Riding a bicycle is 400 times faster**

Top speeds of people and animals

	m/s–ft/s		m/s–ft/s
Pedestrian	1.4/4.62	Swallow	50–60/165–200
Walker	4.19/13.8	Swift	77/254
Runner	10/33	Greenland whale	2/6.6
Skier	35/115.5	Migrating salmon	5/16.5
Swimmer	2/6.6	Horse walking	2/6.6
Rollerskater	11.5/38	Horse trotting	3.75/12.5
Freefall parachutist	279/920	Horse galloping	19.35/64
Dragonfly	6–10/20–33	Elephant	6.5/21.5
Bumble bee	3–5/9.9–16.5	Field hare	20–66
House fly	1.5–2/5–6.6	Kangaroo	17/56
Bee	2.3/7.6	Giraffe	14/46.2
Wasp	1.8/6	House rat	26.8/8.6
Racing pigeon	18–19/60–63		

Average and top speeds

Garden snail
Top speed	0.049 kph = 49 m/h = 0.138 m/s
	0.03 mph = 161 ft/h = 0.05 ft/s
Average speed	0.00058 kph = 0.58 m/h = 58 cm/h
	0.0003 mph = 1.91 ft/h = 23 in/h

Person walking
Top speed	4.19 m/s = 15.1 kph/13.8 ft/s = 9.36 mph
Average speed	1.4 m/s = 5.04 kph/4.62 ft/s = 3.12 mph

Cyclist
Top speed	19.4 m/s = 70 kph/64.02 ft/s = 43.5 mph
Average speed	5.5 m/s = 19.8 kph/18.15 ft/s = 12.25 mph

Horse rider (at a gallop)
Top speed	19.35 m/s = 69.9 kph/64 ft/s = 43.33 mph
Average speed	10 m/s = 36 kph/33 ft/s = 22.32 mph

Comparison of speeds

It is not only man, machine and animal which are on the move. The earth, the sun and the moon are never still.

Orbital speed of the earth around the sun	29.8 km/s/ 18.47 mps
Orbital speed of the moon around the earth	3600 kph/ 2232 mph
Orbital speed of the sun around the center of the Milky Way	250 km/s/ 155 mps

The top speeds of various vehicles

	kph/mph
Apollo 10 (1969)	39,897/24,736
Fastest airplane	3529/2188
Supersonic 'Concorde'	2200/1364
Rocket-driven car	1190/1234
Wheel-driven car	690/428
Speedboat	555.9/344.6
Locomotive engine	330.8/205
Hovercraft	164.6/102
Recommended speed on motorways	112/70
Racing cyclist	70/43.4
Normal cyclist	15–20/10–12.5

Riding a horse is 700 times faster

A car is almost 2000 times faster than the fastest snail

Who gets up first?

Although you can't feel it, the earth is moving all the time. Every 24 hours it revolves once on its own axis. During this time, one half of the earth faces the sun and it is daytime there. The other half lies in shadow and it is night. At the same time as we are getting up in the morning, children in other parts of the world are going to bed. So the earth is divided into time zones. Altogether there are 24 of these time zones. In some countries, however, the actual time shown by the clocks is not always that of the time zone. Otherwise there would be nations, such as the Soviet Union, with 10 different times.

It takes about 7 hours to fly from London to New York. Yet a plane leaving London at 12.00 noon reaches New York at 14.00 that afternoon. It takes approximately 17 hours to fly from London to Tokyo. Yet a plane, also leaving London at noon, will not reach Tokyo until noon the following day. Because of the time difference, it is 5 hours earlier than Central European time in New York, and 9 hours later in Tokyo. These time differences have to be taken into account when working out arrival times. When flying to America, you *deduct* 5–11 hours from the flight time, and when flying to Japan you *add* 9 hours. It becomes even more involved when certain countries, such as Britain, introduce 'summer time'. This means that in the lighter months of the year, ie, in summer, clocks go forward and the day begins one hour earlier than actually corresponds to the time zone. So when booking a long flight, it is advisable to find out when a plane will arrive at its destination – in local time.

In the Soviet Union they have an official time which is different from the standard time. You have to add on one hour to the standard time.

When it is noon in Central Europe, it is: 07.30 in Newfoundland and Suriname: 20.30 in Northern and Southern Australia: 17.30 in Burma and the Cocos Islands: 16.30 in India, Sri Lanka and Nepal: 15.30 in Afghanistan: 14.30 in Iran.

When it is 12 noon in Central Europe, it is . . .

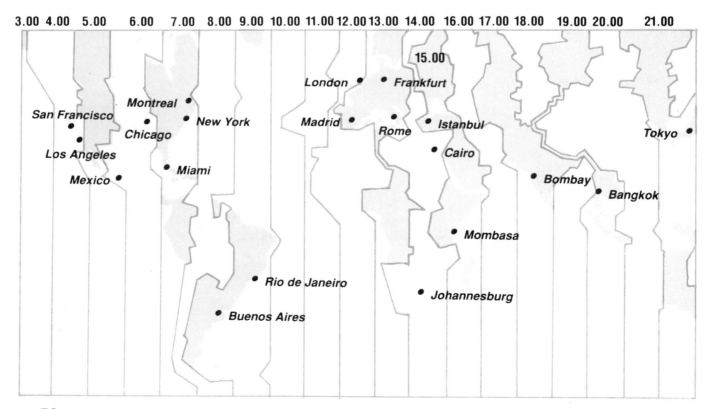

For a South American boy, it is early morning: 07.00 and time to get up . . .

. . . while it is midday and lunchtime for children in Germany . . .

. . . and 19.00 and bedtime for children in China.

What time is it now in other countries? At the same time as children in Germany, for instance, are sitting down to have lunch, usually around midday, children in other countries are either just getting up or getting ready to go to bed. It is time to get up for children in Argentina, Bolivia, Brazil, Chile, Curaçao, Paraguay, Puerto Rico and Venezuela – mostly South and Mid-America; it is 07.00 for them. However, it is bedtime for children in China, Hong Kong, Vietnam, Indonesia, the Philippines, Taiwan and Western Australia; it is 19.00 for them. At the same moment it is 20.00 in Japan and 21.00 in Eastern Australia – time when children should be asleep! When it is 12.00 noon in Germany it is exactly 12 noon in many other countries – Albania, Austria, Belgium, Czechoslovakia, Denmark, France, Holland, Hungary, Italy, Luxembourg, Nigeria, Norway, Poland, Sweden, Switzerland, Spain, Tunisia, Yugoslavia and Zaire (Africa), while in Britain it is still only 11.00.

How long is the shortest year?

The word 'calendar' is derived from the Latin and means the first day of the month. Calendars have been around for many centuries. A calendar can be calculated by the period between one full moon and the next. The first known calendars were based on that period. The proof is that our word 'month' is rather similar to the word 'moon'. A month, if calculated by the phases of the moon, would consist of 29 days, 12 hours and 44 minutes. A year would therefore consist of 365 days, 5 hours and 48 minutes. But because neither the months nor the years could have such odd endings, people tried to find other kinds of calendar. A calendar can also be calculated by the sun, but the solar year also has 365 days, 5 hours and 48 minutes, just as a calendar calculated by the phases of the moon has. The solar calendar can be adjusted by introducing leap years.

The Gregorian calendar, introduced to Rome in 1582 by Pope Gregory, is universally used today, although in many countries it is not the only calendar. The calculation of the new time began with the presumed year of the birth of Jesus Christ. The Gregorian calendar is a solar calendar, and consists of 365 days in a year. The 'extra' hours of the year are made up for by the leap years. Every four years the month of February is longer by one day. Instead of having 28 days it has 29. A leap year has 366 days. You can calculate when a leap year will fall by remembering that the number of the year must be divisible by 4 (1984, 1988). The exception is the turn of the century which must be divisible by 400. The year 1900 was therefore not a leap year, because although divisible by 4 it wasn't divisible by 400. The year 2000 will be a leap year. The Gregorian calendar of today is so exact that a small adjustment will only be necessary in 3000 years.

The Jewish calendar is a mixture of lunar and solar calendar and is rather complicated. The length of the years varies in six different ways, between 353 and 385 days. In addition, there is a 13th month in some years. The Jewish calendar begins with the presumed creation of the world, established as the year 3761 BC. The number of days in each month varies. There are 29 or 30 days. There are also leap years at regular intervals.

The Muslim calendar is a lunar calendar. A new month begins after the new moon. Muslim years have 12 months with 29 and 30 days by turns. The Muslims also have leap years. Their years are 354 or 355 days long. The era of the Muslim calendar begins with the Hejira, when Mohammed migrated from Mecca to Medina in the year 622 AD.

The Maya, an ancient civilization who lived in Central America, also had their own calendar system based on the sun. A year had a total of 365 days, but was divided into 18 rather than 12 months. There were 20 days in each month plus five additional days of evil omen. The calculation of the Maya calendar is very complicated and is contrary to our modern ways of counting. The Maya

In all Christian countries the date of Easter, the Resurrection of Christ, is exactly laid down. It always falls on the first Sunday after the first full moon after the first day of spring. The earliest Easter Sunday can be is 22 March, and the latest is 25 April. The dates of the Easter Sundays until the year 2000 are as follows:

1990:	15 April	1996:	7 April
1991:	31 March	1997:	30 March
1992:	19 April	1998:	12 April
1993:	11 April	1999:	4 April
1994:	3 April	2000:	23 April
1995:	16 April		

also had a day zero because they believed that a day at the beginning of the month wasn't finished yet, therefore it wasn't the first day. The beginning of Maya time is presumed to have been 3114 BC. They measured time by counting all the days from that date (not the years).

The calendar of the Egyptians is a lunar calendar. A year has 12 months with 30 days in each, making 365 days in all. Five additional days act as leap days, the 'Epagomenen', assumed to be days of evil omen. As the ancient Egyptians did not have leap years, the beginning of a new year varied each time. The beginning of the ancient Egyptian era is the first day of the reign of King Nabonassar, on 26 February 747 BC. The calendar of

the ancient Egyptians is not used in modern Egypt.

The calendar of the French Revolution was only valid for 13 years, from 1793 until 1806. It was so new and different that the French Revolutionists found it difficult to persuade the population to use it. It was a solar calendar with 12 months of 30 days each. The missing days were simply added on at the end of the year and were called 'additional days' (jours complémentaires).

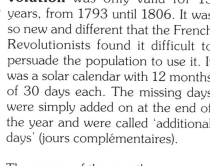

The names of the months were very descriptive; there were the months of rain, blossom, harvest or fruits. Weeks were completely abolished and replaced by periods of ten days called décades. The tenth day of each décade was a holiday like the additional days at the end of the year. The day was divided into 10 hours of 100 decimal minutes with 100 decimal seconds each.

The Chinese and Japanese were introduced to the Gregorian calendar in the 16th century by Jesuit priests who visited the Chinese Imperial court in Peking. Their calendar is different in that the months have no names but are numbered through. The years are also grouped in cycles of 60 years. Each year has 12 months with 29 or 30 days, leap days are built into various months. The year begins in February or March, when the sun is in the sign of Pisces.

Nobody really knows when Jesus Christ was actually born. It was decreed by the abbot Dionysios Exiquus that the beginning of the era should not be based on the founding of Rome but on the birth of Jesus Christ. He assumed Jesus Christ was born in the year 533 of the Julian calendar. The opinion today is that the venerable abbot made a mistake and Christ was born four or seven years earlier than is generally believed.

1 JANUARY 1983

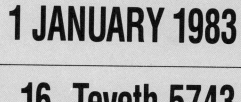 16. Teveth 5743

 16. Rabi-al-awak 1403

 Primidi, 11. Nivose 191

 18th day of 11th month 59th year

 9. Pachin 2731

 12-18-9-10-11- 1 Chuen, 4 Kankin

If all the peoples of the world had retained their original calendar, our New Year's Day would not be a holiday or the beginning of their new year. Take 1 January 1983, for example. In the Chinese calendar the new year starts on 13 February. The Muslims did have a holiday on 1 January 1983, not because it was a new year's day but because it fell on a Saturday, and Fridays and Saturdays are holidays for the Muslims. In France 1 January 1983 was a holiday because, according to the French Revolution calendar it was the anniversary of the French Revolution, the most important holiday of the year. The Gregorian calendar is used in France today, so 1 January is anyway recognized as New Year's Day.

What can carry the most

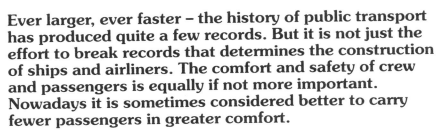

Hindenburg

Ever larger, ever faster – the history of public transport has produced quite a few records. But it is not just the effort to break records that determines the construction of ships and airliners. The comfort and safety of crew and passengers is equally if not more important. Nowadays it is sometimes considered better to carry fewer passengers in greater comfort.

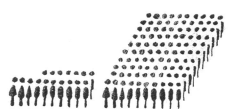

How many people can fit in?	Weight	Speed
Medium-sized car: 5	1000 kg/2205 lb	max. 20 kph/125 mph
Single-decker bus: 39 seats	16t	max 70 kph/45 mph
Taxi: 4	1000 kg/2205 lb	
Double-decker bus: 72 seats	13.8 t	40 kph/25 mph
Single-engine light aircraft: (Cessna 207 Skywagon): 8	1724 kg/3800 lb	256 kph/160 mph
Boeing 747: 219	152 t	960 kph/595 mph
Concorde: 144	185 t	2180 kph/1352 mph
Airbus A 300: 345	158 t	910 kph/564 mph
Boeing 747 'Jumbo': 500	352 t	965 kph/600 mph
DC 10: 380	257 t	910 kph/564 mph
Airship *Hindenburg*: 117	200 t	125 kph/77.5 mph
Steamship *Great Eastern* (1838): 3000		25 kph/15.5 mph
Venetian gondola: 5		5 kph/3 mph
Queen Elizabeth 2: 2025		53 kph/33 mph
United States: 1930		66 kph/41 mph
Railway train *Rocket* (1825): 200		58 kph/36 mph
TGV-PSE (France): 3000		380 kph/235 mph

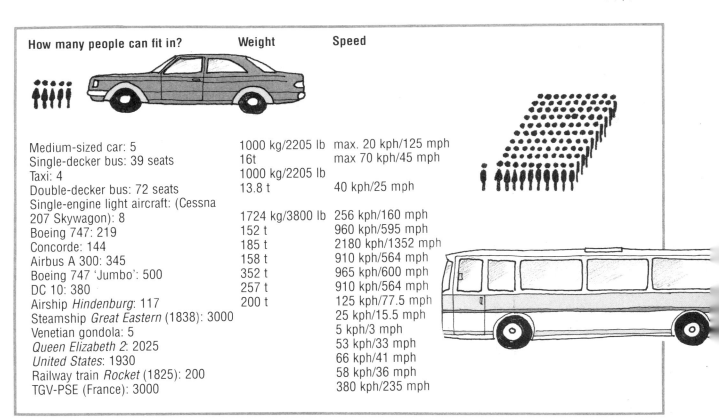

passengers?

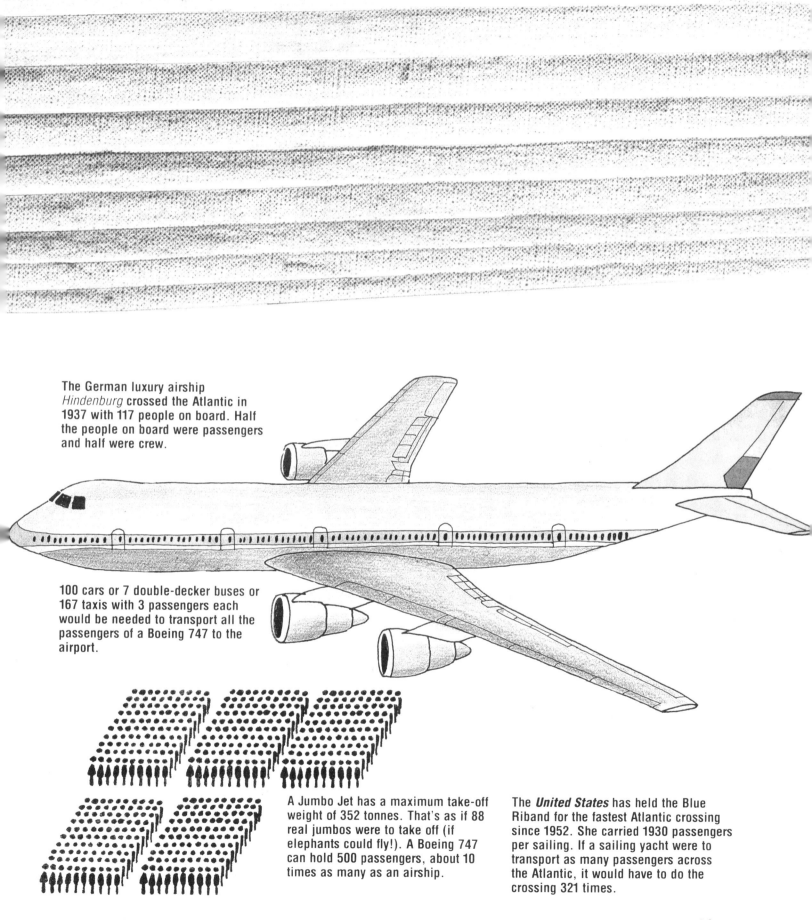

The German luxury airship *Hindenburg* crossed the Atlantic in 1937 with 117 people on board. Half the people on board were passengers and half were crew.

100 cars or 7 double-decker buses or 167 taxis with 3 passengers each would be needed to transport all the passengers of a Boeing 747 to the airport.

A Jumbo Jet has a maximum take-off weight of 352 tonnes. That's as if 88 real jumbos were to take off (if elephants could fly!). A Boeing 747 can hold 500 passengers, about 10 times as many as an airship.

The *United States* has held the Blue Riband for the fastest Atlantic crossing since 1952. She carried 1930 passengers per sailing. If a sailing yacht were to transport as many passengers across the Atlantic, it would have to do the crossing 321 times.

How big is a soccer pitch?

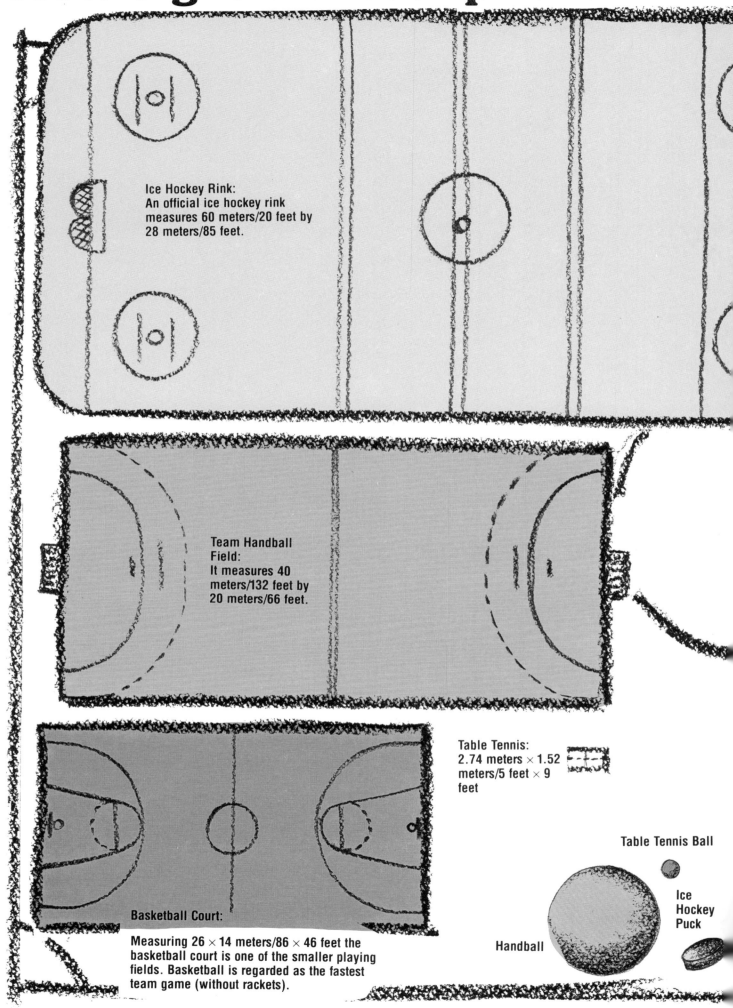

Ice Hockey Rink:
An official ice hockey rink measures 60 meters/20 feet by 28 meters/85 feet.

Team Handball Field:
It measures 40 meters/132 feet by 20 meters/66 feet.

Table Tennis:
2.74 meters × 1.52 meters/5 feet × 9 feet

Basketball Court:
Measuring 26 × 14 meters/86 × 46 feet the basketball court is one of the smaller playing fields. Basketball is regarded as the fastest team game (without rackets).

Table Tennis Ball

Ice Hockey Puck

Handball

People have been playing ball games since the beginning of mankind, but it was as recently as 140 years ago that fixed playing rules were applied all over the world.

One example is football or soccer. Rules for this game were first published around 1848 in England. Rules for team handball have only existed since 1917. The rules of the games also determine the size of the playing area. A basketball player has to run 28 meters/93 feet from one basket to the other, whereas a soccer player must cross up to 120 meters/400 feet to reach the opposite goal, almost four times as far. Compared to a soccer pitch a table tennis table is tiny. You could fit 1750 table tennis tables on to one football pitch, but only 20 basketball courts. You could fit 65 table tennis tables on to a tennis court.

Another game, another ball

Just as important as the playing field and the markings are the size and weight of the ball and the material it is made of. A tennis ball must be heavier than a table tennis ball as it has to fly further and be more wind resistant. Tennis balls are made of rubber covered with felt. The ball is filled with gas. They weigh an average of 58 g/2 oz. A table tennis ball is comparatively light. It only weighs an average of 2.5 g/0.08 oz. The table tennis ball is made of celluloid, a man-made material, and it flies through the air easily. The basketball is made of rubber or plastic because it must be able to bounce well — when it is being dribbled, for example. A good football is made of strong cowhide. It must be resistant to hard kicks and must be able to fly a long way.

Soccer Pitch:
For international matches the required size of a soccer pitch is 110 meters/100 yards by 64–75 meters/70–80 yards.

Basketball

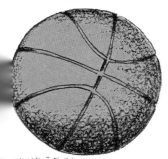

Football

Where is the longest bridge?

Bridges are made of wood, stone, steel, iron, or concrete. The supports and foundations of a bridge must be constructed in such a way that they withstand the pressure of the superstructure and the load it carries. The pressure is borne by different parts of the bridge, depending on its structure. The most important types of bridges are beam or girder, arch and suspension bridges. Tunnels create essential short cuts for modern traffic. The 'project of the century' must be the Channel Tunnel linking Britain and France; completion is expected in the 1990s.

The Romans were building great bridges as early as 300 BC. They constructed aqueducts which carried water across valleys into the cities. Some of these, such as the Pont du Gard near Nîmes in France, are still in good condition today. This aqueduct is an arch bridge built of stone. The more arches a bridge has, the stronger it is. The span of a suspension bridge is much greater than that of an arch bridge. The span is the distance between the bridge supports.

The largest concrete arch bridge in the world is the Krk Island bridge in Yugoslavia which has a span of 390 meters/1287 feet.

The span of suspension bridges can reach more than 1000 meters/3300 feet. The suspension bridge with the greatest span, 1780 meters/5874 feet, was built in 1987 between Honshu and Shikoku in Japan. The largest single-span suspension bridge is the Humber Estuary Bridge in England. It is 1410 meters/4626 feet long with a span of 2200 meters/7260 feet.

A suspension bridge made of iron was first built in England in 1741. It was 21 meters/70 feet long. The Chicago-Alton Railway Bridge across the Missouri in the USA, built in 1878, was the first bridge to be constructed entirely of steel. The longest steel arch bridge was completed in 1977. It spans 518.2 meters/1710 feet across the New River Gorge in the USA. Even greater spans can be achieved using steel-reinforced concrete. The Quebec Bridge across the St Lawrence River was first opened in 1917. It has an overall length of 853 meters/2815 feet and a span of 549 meters/1800 feet. The highest bridge in Europe is the Europa Bridge on the Kufstein-Brenner Pass in Austria. It is 190 meters/627 feet high, 820 meters/2706 feet long and 34 meters/112 feet wide. It also has the highest bridge supports in Europe. They are made of steel-reinforced concrete and are 181 meters (597 feet) high.

The first types of bridges were tree trunks laid across a river or festoons of creeper plants suspended between trees. Bridges made of wood are only used as temporary constructions nowadays. Their span seldom exceeds 50 meters (165 feet).

Tunnel Builders. The Romans were also pioneers in tunneling. The first tunnels served as irrigation and drainage systems. During the middle of the first century the Romans built a tunnel 5.6 km/3½ miles long to drain Lake Fucinus. With the discovery of gunpowder in the 17th century great masses of rock could be blasted away and longer tunnels could be built. The

Bridges and tunnels

Malpas Tunnel for the Languedoc Canal, built in France in 1679–81, measured 157 meters/515 feet, for example. With the introduction of the railway at the beginning of the 19th century, more and more tunnels were built. But it was the invention of dynamite in 1867 that made the construction of the large tunnels through mountains possible. Later gigantic ram air compressors were installed as well. The longest railway tunnel in the world is the Seikan tunnel in Japan, which is 54 km/33½ miles long.

The Romans built the Pont du Gard near Nîmes in France in the 1st century BC. This aqueduct is 48 meters/158 feet high, as high as a modern highrise building with 16 storeys.

Great Bridges of the World Bridge	Length (m/ft)	Completed
Humber Estuary Bridge (UK) (largest suspension bridge)	1410/4626	1981
Quebec Railway Bridge (Canada) (largest steel bridge)	853/1800	1917
Sydney Harbour Bridge (Australia) (longest steel arch bridge)	495/1652	1932
Second Lake Pontchartrain (USA) (longest bridging)	38,422/126,055	1969
Royal Gorge, Colorado (USA) (world's highest bridge) height: 321 m/1053 ft	268/880	1929
Europa Bridge (Austria) (highest bridge in Europe) height: 190 m/627 ft	820/2706	1963

How hot is it at the equator?

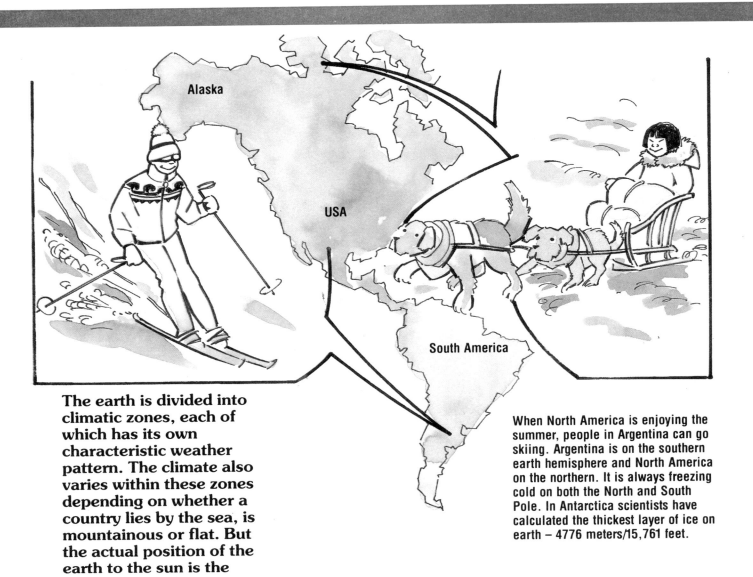

The earth is divided into climatic zones, each of which has its own characteristic weather pattern. The climate also varies within these zones depending on whether a country lies by the sea, is mountainous or flat. But the actual position of the earth to the sun is the most relevant factor.

When North America is enjoying the summer, people in Argentina can go skiing. Argentina is on the southern earth hemisphere and North America on the northern. It is always freezing cold on both the North and South Pole. In Antarctica scientists have calculated the thickest layer of ice on earth – 4776 meters/15,761 feet.

Temperature rises above 90°F/33°C in the summer are considered quite extreme in the countries of Central Europe. They are quite normal in Ethiopia, however. The village of Dallol is the hottest place on earth. The yearly average temperature there is 95°F/35°C. The coldest place on earth is Antarctica where scientists have recorded an average temperature of −72°F/−57.8°C. The Ethiopian village of Dallol is in the tropics, the hottest climatic zone on earth. The tropics encircle the earth like a belt. The countries near the equator are always hot during the day because the sun's rays are at their most intensive there. This is the case the whole year round, so there is no change of season. At both cold poles of the earth the sun's

rays are most diffused and the curvature of the earth's surface is most noticeable. The rays of the sun can hardly warm the countries around the North and South poles.

The Eastern Sahara lies at the equator and is the sunniest place on earth. The sun burns down on the sand for 355 days of the year. At the North Pole, however, the sun seldom shines. The periods of winter when there is no sun at all can last up to 186 days. The lowest temperature ever recorded was registered in the Antarctic. On 21 July 1983 the temperature dropped to −128.6°F/−89.2°C. The hottest day on record was on 13 September 1922 in Aziziyah, Libya, when the temperature climbed to 136.4°F/58.0°C.

The coldest month in Britain is January when the average temperature in London is 39.2°F/4°C. In the Argentinian capital of Buenos Aires, on the other hand, the average temperature for the month of January is 74.3°F/23.5°C. This is due to the fact that the earth's axis is not vertical as it orbits the sun. The seasons change because the earth's axis is inclined to one side. On its journey around the sun, first the southern half of the earth is nearer the sun and then the northern half is.

Temperature

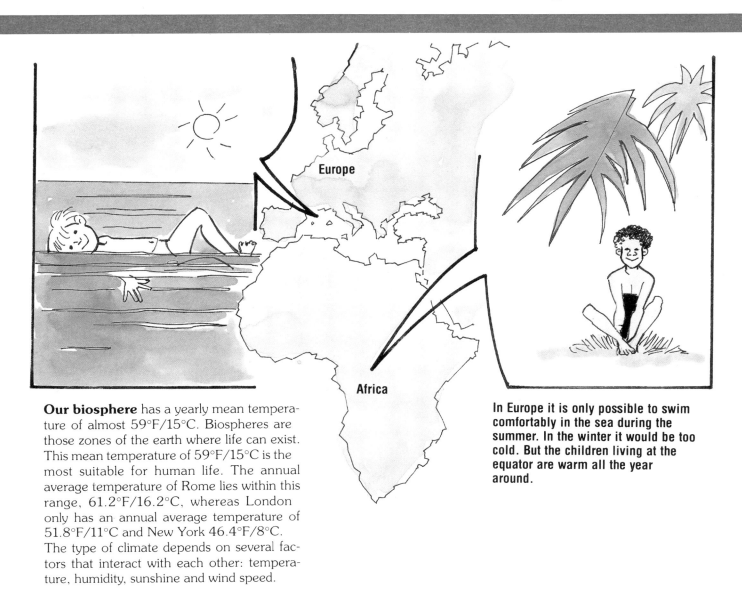

Europe

Africa

Our biosphere has a yearly mean temperature of almost 59°F/15°C. Biospheres are those zones of the earth where life can exist. This mean temperature of 59°F/15°C is the most suitable for human life. The annual average temperature of Rome lies within this range, 61.2°F/16.2°C, whereas London only has an annual average temperature of 51.8°F/11°C and New York 46.4°F/8°C. The type of climate depends on several factors that interact with each other: temperature, humidity, sunshine and wind speed.

In Europe it is only possible to swim comfortably in the sea during the summer. In the winter it would be too cold. But the children living at the equator are warm all the year around.

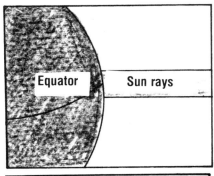

Equator | Sun rays

North Pole

Sun rays

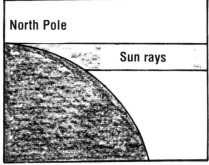

Why is the sun most intensive at the equator and least intensive at the poles? Here is a simple test:

Direct the beam of a flash light horizontally on to a piece of white cardboard. The light spot will be small but very bright (like the sun's rays at the equator).

When the cardboard is tilted slightly backwards the light spot becomes bigger but also paler (like the sun's rays at the poles).

89

How big is the earth?

When Christopher Columbus sailed from Spain to the New World it took him more than 10 weeks. Today we can fly the same distance in just a few hours. The world has become smaller, or so it's said. Of course, it hasn't really become smaller. It's just that our means of transport have become faster.

The fastest airplane can fly more than 2100 km/130 miles per hour. Concorde needs only three hours to cross the Atlantic. Trains, too, have become faster and faster. The 'Tokaido' train between the two Japanese cities of Okayama and Osaka is able to race through the land at speeds of 210 km/130 miles per hour. British Rail operates trains at speeds of 160 km/100 miles per hour. Very high-speed train operations have also been introduced in France where the TGV-PSE can travel at top speeds of 380 km/235 miles per hour between Paris and Lyons. And the United States Metroliners are capable of running at up to 260 km/160 miles per hour.

Distance cannot always be measured accurately. If you are looking at a distant hill, you may wonder how far away it is but unless you have a map you cannot be sure. You can estimate the distance, however, by working out how far you can see. The calculation is based on the height you are standing at; the higher you are, the further you can see. (You need a clear day for this, of course.)

Range of visibility	
Eye height m/ft	Visibility km/miles
2/6½	5.4/3
5/16½	8.6/5
10/33	12.1/7½
15/49½	15/9
20/66	17/10½
50/165	27/17
100/330	38.3/24
200/660	55/34
400/1320	77/47½
600/1980	94/58
800/2640	114.8/71
1000/3300	121/75
1500/4950	148.2/92
2000/6600	171.1/106
3000/9900	209.6/130
4000/13,200	242/150
8000/26,400	342.3/212
9000/29,700	363/225

What is the flight time to the large cities of the world?

km/miles

London to:
New York	5536/3432	= 6:50 h
Buenos Aires	11,129/6900	= 18:45 h
Johannesburg	9067/5622	= 16:25 h
Sydney	17,000/10,540	= 24:00 h
Tokyo	9548/5942	= 17:00 h

New York to:
Buenos Aires	8539/5294	= 12:40 h
Johannesburg	12,822/7950	= 20:30 h
Sydney	16,000/9920	= 35:00 h
Tokyo	10,870/6740	= 15:40 h

Buenos Aires to:
Johannesburg	8100/5022	= 13:25 h
Sydney	11,755/7288	= 17:10 h
Tokyo	18,340/11,371	= 39:35 h

Johannesburg to:
Sydney	11,020/6832	= 17:10 h
Tokyo	13,515/8379	= 21:15 h

Sydney to:
Tokyo	7812/4843	= 9:45 h

Munich to:
London	946/586	= 2:00 h
New York	6188/3836	= 8:45 h
Buenos Aires	13,247/8213	= 14:50 h
Johannesburg	9228/5721	= 10:55 h
Sydney	19,036/11,802	= 21:40 h
Tokyo	13,840/8580	= 16:10 h

The scale of a map can be illustrated by comparing it with a photograph. The farther away you stand to take the picture, the more you can get in but everything is small and you cannot see detail. A small-scale map covers a large area but there is not much detail. A close-up picture shows less of the scene but in more detail. The same is true of a large-scale map.

scale 1:1,000,000

scale 1:100,000

Distances

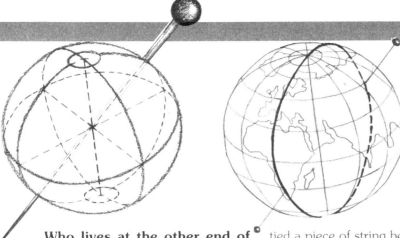

Who lives at the other end of the world? If you could drop a plumb line from the spot you are standing on down a hole through the center of the earth, it would reappear exactly at the other side and it would be antipodal. The word 'antipode' comes from Greek-Latin and means opposite feet. An antipode is a person living at the opposite side of the earth. Britain's antipodes are the people from New Zealand. The other end of the earth is 21,000 km/13,000 miles away if you travel along the surface (the earth's circumference). If you went right through the earth, the antipodes would be between 12,712 km/7880 miles (double the radius of the equator) and 12,754 km/7907 miles (the axis of the earth) away.

How is the distance between two cities measured? The shortest distance between two points on the earth is measured by means of the 'great circle line'. If you marked two points on a globe with pins and tied a piece of string between them, you would get the 'great circle line'. You could not rely on the great circle line to plan a travel route, however, because it cuts through mountains, lakes and cities. The difference between the great circle line and the actual distance you have to travel can be quite considerable.

Distance	Great circle km/miles	Actual distance km/miles
Paris–Berlin	871/540	1072/637
Rome–Berlin	1181/732	1541/955
Rome–London	1427/885	1897/1176
London–Moscow	2493/1546	2966/1839

You can calculate the **distance between two places** accurately by using a map. The scale of the map is always given for this reason.

The map scale refers to the size of the place as shown on the map compared with its actual size. The larger the second figure of the scale, the smaller the scale of the map. Thus 1:1,000,000 is a smaller scale than 1:100,000.

The scale chosen for a map depends what it is to be used for. A map of the world has a very small scale such as 1:1,000,000 because the entire earth has to be fitted on to it. A road map has a larger scale so that all the roads, squares, forests, rivers, railway lines and so on can be seen. Maps for walkers or ordnance survey maps have an even larger scale. They show details like churches, bridges, footpaths, canals and castles.

The scale of a map is shown somewhere on the edge. It is usually given in cm/km or inches/miles.

scale 1:10,000

scale 1:1000

Wonders of the world

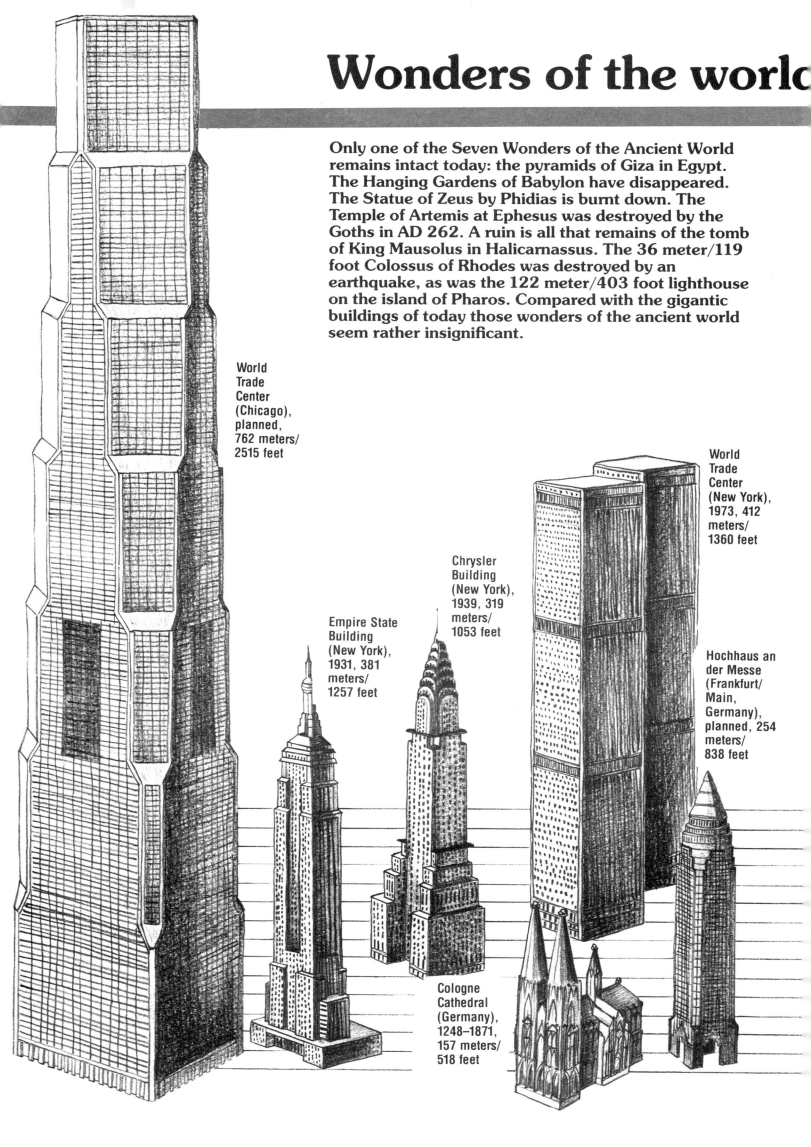

Only one of the Seven Wonders of the Ancient World remains intact today: the pyramids of Giza in Egypt. The Hanging Gardens of Babylon have disappeared. The Statue of Zeus by Phidias is burnt down. The Temple of Artemis at Ephesus was destroyed by the Goths in AD 262. A ruin is all that remains of the tomb of King Mausolus in Halicarnassus. The 36 meter/119 foot Colossus of Rhodes was destroyed by an earthquake, as was the 122 meter/403 foot lighthouse on the island of Pharos. Compared with the gigantic buildings of today those wonders of the ancient world seem rather insignificant.

World Trade Center (Chicago), planned, 762 meters/ 2515 feet

World Trade Center (New York), 1973, 412 meters/ 1360 feet

Chrysler Building (New York), 1939, 319 meters/ 1053 feet

Empire State Building (New York), 1931, 381 meters/ 1257 feet

Hochhaus an der Messe (Frankfurt/ Main, Germany), planned, 254 meters/ 838 feet

Cologne Cathedral (Germany), 1248–1871, 157 meters/ 518 feet

Some records

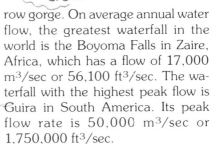

The highest office building in the world is the Sears Tower in Chicago (USA), which is 443 meters/1462 feet high and has 110 storeys. If you include the television tower at the top, the Empire State building in New York is 449 meters/1482 feet high. The building itself is only 381 meters/1257 feet (102 storeys) high. The highest residential building is the Lake Point Tower in Chicago, 197 meters/650 feet and 70 storeys. The tallest office block in Britain is the National Westminster tower in London which is 183 meters/600 feet and 49 storeys high. The tallest church spire in the world is at the Cathedral of Ulm in Germany. It is 161 meters/528 high.

The American building company Trump is planning several giant houses, though work on them has not yet begun. They should be up to 762 meters/2515 feet high.

A truly natural wonder is **Ayer's Rock in Australia**. A gigantic rock (monolith) seems to emerge suddenly from the totally flat desert. Rising 860 meters/2845 feet above sea level, the rock is is 6 km/4 miles long, 348 meters/1143 feet high and measures 9 km/5½ miles around its base.

The giant rocks of **Stonehenge**, in Great Britain, which were erected by people thousands of years ago, are still shrouded in mystery. Two gigantic blocks of stone weighing 45 tonnes each, stand upright with another smaller block lying across the top. Several of these 'horseshoes' form a large circle. There must have been at least 500 men carrying these stones more than 4500 years ago.

The waves through which the American Navy Lieutenant Frederic Margraff sailed with his ship in 1933 when it was hit by an enormous hurricane, were as high as 25 children. A giant wave almost pulled him and his ship down into the depths of the ocean. Margraff calculated the height of that wave at 34 meters/112 feet.

Wonders of nature: waterfalls. It is rather difficult to calculate the height of a waterfall. Taking the height is not always easy because some waterfalls plunge straight down and others fall down over several steps; they are called cataracts. Taking the amount of water that falls down each year doesn't provide an accurate basis for calculation, either. Some waterfalls dry up during certain seasons. Perhaps one should take the most beautiful or impressive waterfall?

The highest waterfall in the world is the Angel Falls in Venezuela with two steps and a total drop of 979 meters/3212 feet. Perhaps the most beautiful waterfall is the Iguaçu Falls. This cataract consists of 22 larger and 250 smaller falls between 57 and 72 meters/188 and 238 feet deep. At the top, the river is more than 2.5 km/1½ miles wide and the water falls over two steps into a narrow gorge. On average annual water flow, the greatest waterfall in the world is the Boyoma Falls in Zaire, Africa, which has a flow of 17,000 m³/sec or 56,100 ft³/sec. The waterfall with the highest peak flow is Guira in South America. Its peak flow rate is 50,000 m³/sec or 1,750,000 ft³/sec.

A total of about 14,000 m³/sec or 500,000 ft³/sec thunder down the Augrabies Falls of the Orange River in South Africa, which has a drop of 150 meters/500 feet. The highest waterfall in Great Britain is the Eas-Coul-Aulin in Scotland with a drop of 200 meters/658 feet.

A very regular worker is the Old Faithful geyser: every 63 minutes or so it erupts with a hot water fountain 40 meters/100 feet or more high. The tallest geyser was probably the Waimangu geyser in New Zealand. It erupted with a 100 meter/330 foot high water fountain for the first time in 1909. Its tallest fountain was an unbelievable 457 meters/1508 feet high. It has been dormant since 1917.

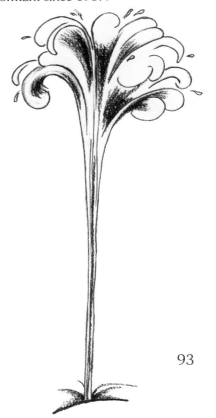

The Seven Wonders of the World		
	Location	Built
The Pyramids of Giza	El Gizeh, Egypt	approx 2580–1650 BC
The Hanging Gardens of Semiramis in Babylon	Babylon, Iraq	about 626 BC
The Temple of Artemis	Ephesus, Turkey	about 650 BC
The Statue of Zeus by Phidias	Olympia, Greece	about 430 BC
The Tomb of King Mausolus of Caria	Halicarnassus (Bodrum), Turkey	about 350 BC
The Colossus of Rhodes	Rhodes, Greece	292–280 BC
The Lighthouse of the Island of Pharos	near Alexandria, Egypt	283 BC

In the Middle Ages (about 700 years ago), a group of houses was classed as a town if there were between 500 and 1000 inhabitants. Today it would be called a village. Towns are classified according to the number of people who live there. A small country town has 2000–5000 inhabitants. The medium-sized market town may have 5000–20,000 inhabitants. A large town often has well over 100,000 people living in it. A city is a town which is important in some way, though not necessarily because of its size. It may be important because it has a cathedral, or because it is a seat of local or national government.

Some cities are far bigger than others, of course. A huge city is called a metropolis. The word comes from two Greek words meaning 'mother' and 'city', and the metropolis is often the chief city or capital of a country. A metropolis is a city with more than 1 million inhabitants. There are two metropolitan cities in Britain: London, which has a population of 7,168,000, and Birmingham, which has 1,003,000 inhabitants. North America has several metropolitan cities. The biggest are New York (11,571,000 people), Los Angeles (7,032,000 people) and Philadelphia (4,818,000 people).

It is not only the number of inhabitants which has to be considered when comparing the size of cities. The total area covered by the town is relevant too. The town with the largest area in the world is Mount Isa, in Queensland, Australia. It measures 40,978 km²/15,572 miles². London is Britain's largest city as far as population is concerned. It also covers the largest area. Greater London has an area of 1604.4 km²/609.7 miles². When you consider how many people live on a square km/mile, London is not nearly as crowded as some cities. In Mexico City, for example, more than twice as many people live in just under the same amount of space. This includes all the suburbs and shanty towns on the outskirts of the city. The total population of Greater Mexico City is 17,321,000 and the population of the inner city itself is 10,499,000. It is thought that there may be over 31,000,000 people living in Mexico City by the year 2000. The most densely populated city area in the world is the Keihin Metropolitan Area (the Tokyo-Yokohama Metropolitan Area) in Japan. Here, nearly 30,000,000 live in an area of 2800 km²/1081 miles².

The most heavily populated country in the world is China. It is estimated that 1,085,000,000 people live there and this is increasing by over 35,000 people a day, or nearly 13 million a year. The most densely populated territory in the world is Macao, which is also in China. Here, 392,000 people live in an area of 16.05 km²/6.2 miles². This works out at 24,423 people per km², or 63,225 people per mile². Of the larger territories, the most heavily populated is Hong Kong, where 5,533,000 people live in an area of 1037 km²/400.5 miles² (5169 people per km², or 13,390 per mile²).

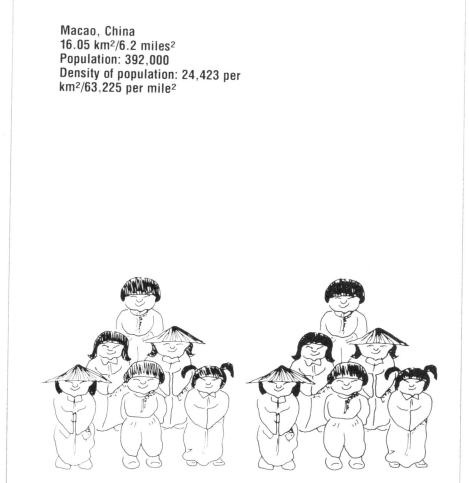

Macao, China
16.05 km²/6.2 miles²
Population: 392,000
Density of population: 24,423 per km²/63,225 per mile²

Growth of world population	
Date	**Millions**
8000 BC	about 6
AD 1	about 255
1000	about 254
1500	460
1700	680
1900	1633
1950	2513
1960	3050
1970	3678
1980	4420
1988	5082

Keihin Metropolitan Area, Tokyo-Yokohama, Japan
2800 km^2/1081 miles^2
Population: 30,000,000
Density of population: 10,714 per km^2/17,752 per mile^2

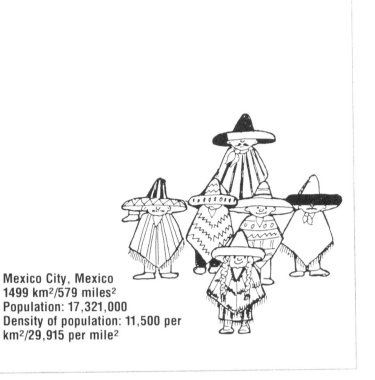

Mexico City, Mexico
1499 km^2/579 miles^2
Population: 17,321,000
Density of population: 11,500 per km^2/29,915 per mile^2

London, England
1604 km^2/609.7 miles^2
Population: 7,168,000
Density of population: 4468 per km^2/11,750 per mile^2

Hong Kong
1037 km^2/400.5 miles^2
Population: 5,533,000
Density of population: 5169 per km^2/13,390 per mile^2

A whole country is never so densely populated as a town because fewer people live in the country areas. The most densely populated large country is Bangladesh. Here, 103,200,000 people live on an area of 142,775 km^2/55,126 miles^2. This makes the density of the population 727 per km^2/1882 per mile^2.

95

How big is North America?

North America is the third largest continent in the world. It is bordered by the Arctic Ocean to the north, the Pacific Ocean to the west, the Atlantic Ocean to the east, and the Isthmus of Panama to the south. North America, which includes the area known as Central America, consists of three main countries, Canada, the United States, and Mexico, together with the island of Greenland, the West Indies, and the countries of Central America.

The total area of the North American continent is 24,900,000 km²/9,600,000 miles². It is 7200 km/4500 miles from north to south, and 6400 km/4000 miles from west to east at the widest part. It contains two of the largest countries in the world, Canada (9,976,139 km²/3,851,809 miles²) and the United States (9,363,353 km²/3,615,211 miles²).

The United States of America consists of the central part of the continent with the addition of Alaska in the north-west and the islands of Hawaii, which are in the Pacific Ocean. It is made up of 50 states. Each state has its own laws, governor and government, but the whole country is controlled by the federal government in Washington D.C. The USA has more than 50 cities with populations of more than 250,000. After New York, the largest cities are Chicago, Illinois; Los Angeles, California; Philadelphia, Pennsylvania; and Detroit, Michigan.

The country is so big that people fly from state to state by airplane, and all the major cities are linked by internal airlines. There are 5,000,000 km/3,000,000 miles of road and 320,000 km/200,000 miles of railway track. America also makes use of waterways for transporting people and goods. The St

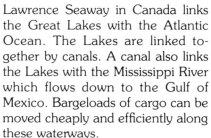

Lawrence Seaway in Canada links the Great Lakes with the Atlantic Ocean. The Lakes are linked together by canals. A canal also links the Lakes with the Mississippi River which flows down to the Gulf of Mexico. Bargeloads of cargo can be moved cheaply and efficiently along these waterways.

Geographic facts

The states of the United States

The states are grouped in seven regions. The table shows the name of each state with its abbreviation, and its capital city.

State	Capital city	State	Capital city	State	Capital city
NEW ENGLAND				**SOUTH-WESTERN STATES**	
Connecticut (Conn)	Hartford	North Dakota (ND)	Bismarck	Oklahoma (Okla)	Oklahoma City
Maine (Me)	Augusta	Ohio (O)	Columbus	Texas (Tex)	Austin
Massachusetts (Mass)	Boston	South Dakota (SD)	Pierre		
New Hampshire (NH)	Concord	Wisconsin (Wis)	Madison	**ROCKY MOUNTAIN STATES**	
Rhode Island (RI)	Providence			Arizona (Ariz)	Phoenix
Vermont (Vt)	Montpelier			Colorado (Colo)	Denver
				Idaho (Ida)	Boise
MIDDLE ATLANTIC STATES		**SOUTHERN STATES**		Montana (Mont)	Helena
		Alabama (Ala)	Montgomery	Nevada (Nev)	Carson City
New Jersey (NJ)	Trenton	Arkansas (Ark)	Little Rock	New Mexico (N.Mex)	Santa Fe
New York (NY)	Albany	Delaware (Del)	Dover	Utah (Ut)	Salt Lake City
Pennsylvania (Penn)	Harrisburg	Florida (Fla)	Tallahassee	Wyoming (Wyo)	Cheyenne
		Georgia (Ga)	Atlanta		
MIDWESTERN STATES		Kentucky (Ky)	Frankfort	**PACIFIC COAST STATES**	
Illinois (Ill)	Springfield	Louisiana (La)	Baton Rouge	California (Calif)	Sacramento
Indiana (Ind)	Indianapolis	Maryland (Md)	Annapolis	Oregon (Ore)	Salem
Iowa (Ia)	Des Moines	Mississippi (Miss)	Jackson	Washington (Wash)	Olympia
Kansas (Kan)	Topeka	North Carolina (NC)	Raleigh		
Michigan (Mich)	Lansing	South Carolina (SC)	Columbia	**OTHERS**	
Minnesota (Minn)	St Paul	Tennessee (Tenn)	Nashville	Alaska	Juneau
Missouri (Mo)	Jefferson City	Virginia (Va)	Richmond	Hawaii	Honolulu
Nebraska (Nebr)	Lincoln	West Virginia (W.Va)	Charleston		

Which is the biggest country in

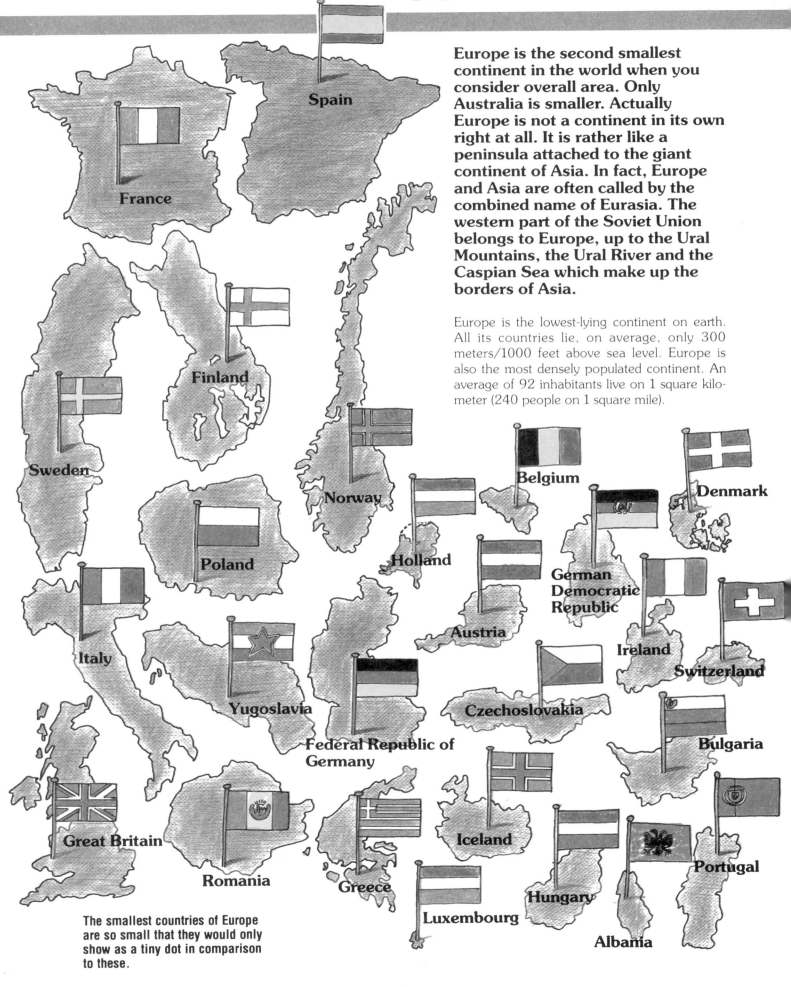

Europe is the second smallest continent in the world when you consider overall area. Only Australia is smaller. Actually Europe is not a continent in its own right at all. It is rather like a peninsula attached to the giant continent of Asia. In fact, Europe and Asia are often called by the combined name of Eurasia. The western part of the Soviet Union belongs to Europe, up to the Ural Mountains, the Ural River and the Caspian Sea which make up the borders of Asia.

Europe is the lowest-lying continent on earth. All its countries lie, on average, only 300 meters/1000 feet above sea level. Europe is also the most densely populated continent. An average of 92 inhabitants live on 1 square kilometer (240 people on 1 square mile).

Spain

France

Finland

Sweden

Norway

Poland

Holland

Belgium

Denmark

German Democratic Republic

Austria

Ireland

Switzerland

Italy

Yugoslavia

Czechoslovakia

Bulgaria

Federal Republic of Germany

Great Britain

Iceland

Portugal

Romania

Greece

Hungary

Luxembourg

Albania

The smallest countries of Europe are so small that they would only show as a tiny dot in comparison to these.

The countries of Europe in order of size

Country	Area in km²/miles²	Inhabitants in millions	Population per km²/miles²	Capital	Inhabitants in thousands
Soviet Union (Europe part)	5,571,000/2,150,406	186.31	8.3/3	Moscow	7628
France (F)	547,026/211,152	55.06	100/38	Paris	9108
Spain (E)	504,782/194,845	38.23	76/29	Madrid	3727
Sweden (S)	449,964/173,686	8.33	19/7	Stockholm	1350
Finland (SF)	337,009/130,085	4.88	14.4/5	Helsinki	845
Norway (N)	324,219/125,148	3.98	12/4	Oslo	469
Poland (PL)	312,677/120,693	36.57	117/45	Warsaw	1630
Italy (I)	310,262/119,761	56.84	188/72	Rome	2922
West Germany (D)	284,686/109,888	62.04	250/96	Bonn	283
Yugoslavia (YU)	256,000/98,816	22.86	89.4/34	Belgrade	1204
Great Britain (GB)	244,046/94,201	56.11	229/88	London	7168
Romania (RO)	237,500/91,675	22.7	95.6/37	Bucharest	1959
Greece (GR)	131,944/50,930	9.85	74.7/29	Athens	885
Czechoslovakia (CS)	127,881/49,362	15.42	121/47	Prague	1183
East Germany (DDR)	108,333/41,816	16.69	154/59	East Berlin	1173
Iceland (IS)	103,000/39,758	0.24	2.3/.89	Reykjavik	83
Bulgaria (BG)	100,912/38,952	8.95	81/31 ·	Sofia	1083
Hungary (H)	93,032/35,910	10.71	114/44	Budapest	2072
Portugal (P)	92,082/35,543	10.11	110/42	Lisbon	812
Austria (A)	83,853/32,367	7.57	90/35	Vienna	1505
Irish Republic (IRL)	70,283/27,129	3.51	50/19	Dublin	543
Denmark (DK)	43,069/16,624	5.13	119/46	Copenhagen	1378
Switzerland (CH)	41,293/15,939	6.48	157/60	Berne	283
Netherlands (NL)	40,844/15,765	14.39	346/133	Amsterdam	1002
Belgium (B)	30,513/11,778	9.86	323/124	Brussels	1075
Albania (AL)	28,748/11,096	2.84	99/38	Tirana	175
Turkey (Europe part)	24,378/9,409	5.75	235/91	Ankara	2200
Luxembourg (L)	2,548/983	360,000	139/53	Luxembourg	75
Andorra (AND)	453/175	40,000	88/34	Andorra la Vella	13
Malta (M)	316/122	380,000	1204/465	Valletta	14
Liechtenstein (FL)	157/60	30,000	191/74	Vaduz	4
San Marino (RSM)	61/23	20,206	366/141	San Marino	20
Monaco (MC)	1.5/0.6	27,063	14,243/5498	Monaco-ville	2
Vatican (V)	0.4/0.15	392	11,725/4526	Vatican	0.39

(in brackets: International Registration Sign)

The total area of Europe (including the Soviet Union west of the Ural) covers 9,699,000 km²/3,782,710 miles². The part belonging to the USSR has the largest area (5,571,000 km²/2,172,692 miles²). But as this part of the USSR is not an independent state, France (547,026 km²/213,340 miles²) is considered to be Europe's largest country.

Many different languages are spoken in Europe. In North America, English is the main language, but a European would have to speak around 70 different languages to be able to communicate adequately with all the other Europeans.

The countries of Europe showing their relative sizes.

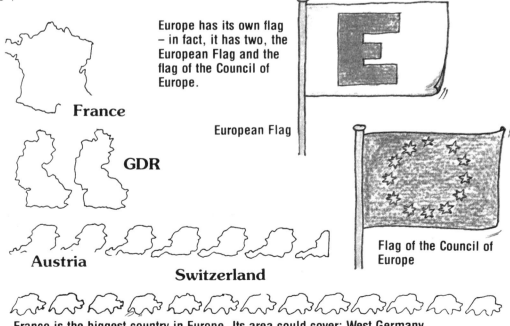

France

GDR

Austria

Switzerland

Europe has its own flag – in fact, it has two, the European Flag and the flag of the Council of Europe.

European Flag

Flag of the Council of Europe

France is the biggest country in Europe. Its area could cover: West Germany twice, Austria 6.5 times and Switzerland 13 times.

Which is the biggest continent?

Only about a third of the surface of the earth is covered by land (29 per cent or 148.3 million km²/57.8 million miles²). These masses of land are divided into seven continents: Asia, Africa, Europe, Australia, North America (including Central America), South America and uninhabited Antarctica. Asia is the largest of these continents. It has 30 per cent of the entire land mass (44.5 million km²/17.3 million miles²). If Europe was included with Asia instead of being thought of as a separate continent, that would be 37 per cent (or 54.5 million km²/21.2 million miles²).

The continents of the world	
	km²/miles
Asia	44.5 mill/17.3 mill
America	42.0 mill/16.4 mill
Africa	30.3 mill/11.8 mill
Europe	9.9 mill/3.9 mill
Australia	8.5 mill/3.3 mill

Some comparisons: The entire area of Asia could easily cover the moon which has a total area of 37,960,000 km²/14,804,400 miles². America, too, would be big enough to cover the moon, but Africa would need to be 20 per cent bigger than it is, whereas Europe is so small that it would need to be four times bigger to cover the area of the moon. Australia would have to be five times bigger.

Europe is not actually an independent continent. It could be seen as an 'extension' of Asia and both continents are often combined as Eurasia. The border between the two continents is marked by mountains, large rivers and lakes and runs along the Ural Mountains, the River Ural, across the Caucasus, through the Black Sea down to the Mediterranean.

Asia is a continent of records. It borders all three oceans of the earth. The biggest lake, the Caspian Sea, and the deepest fresh-water lake, Lake Baikal, both lie in Asia. The highest mountain range, the Himalayas, is also in Asia and it contains the highest mountain on earth, Mount Everest. With an average height of 925 meters/3025 feet above sea level, Asia is the highest continent. And it also contains the deepest water on earth – the Marianas Trench in the Pacific Ocean (11,000 meters/36,300 feet) provides the deepest rut in the crust of the earth.

As the Marianas Trench is the deepest depression in the sea, the deepest hollow on land is the Dead Sea. The level of the Dead Sea lies about 400 meters/1320 feet below the normal sea level and therefore provides the deepest natural 'dip' on the surface of the earth.

The greatest temperature fluctuations also occur on the Asiatic continent, mainly in Siberia. The coldest place on earth is found here too. The most people live in Asia. Fifty-eight out of every 100 people in the world are Asian.

How many times can the countries of Europe fit on the moon?		
Country	Area in km²/miles²	How many times the area of the moon?
Austria	83,849/32,365	452
Belgium	30,513/11,778	1244
Denmark	43,069/16,624	881
Finland	337,009/130,085	112
France	547,026/211,152	69
Germany (East)	108,180/41,757	350
Germany (West)	248,667/95,985	152
Great Britain and Northern Ireland	244,046/94,201	155
Greece	131,944/50,930	287
Iceland	103,300/39,873	386
Italy	301,225/116,272	117
Holland	40,855/15,770	929
Norway	324,219/125,148	117
Spain (incl. Balearics)	504,782/194,845	75
Sweden	449,964/173,686	84
Switzerland	41,288/15,937	919

Continents

The surface of the earth

Total:	510 million km²/197 million miles²
Land area:	(29%) 148.3 million km²/57.2 million miles²
Sea area:	(71%) 363 million k²/140 million miles²
Circumference of the earth:	40,000 km/25,000 miles
Surface of the moon:	37.96 million km²/14.6 million miles²
Circumference of the moon:	10,895 km/6,755 miles

How many times can the largest countries of the earth fit on the moon?

Country	Area in km²/ miles²	How many times the area of the moon?
USSR	22,402,200/8,647,249	1.6
Canada	9,976,139/3,850,789	3.8
China	9,560,980/3,690,538	4
USA	9,363,123/3,614,165	4
Brazil	8,511,965/3,285,618	4.5
Australia	7,686,848/2,967,123	4.9
India	3,287,590/1,269,009	11.5
Argentina	2,776,889/1,071,879	13.6
Sudan	2,505,813/967,243	15.1
Zaire	2,345,405/905,326	16.1

In comparison, Great Britain and Northern Ireland can be fitted on to the moon 155 times, France 69 times and Switzerland 919 times.

The Great Wall of China has a total length of 2,710 km/1,684 miles. It would have to be just over four times as long to go around the moon once (the moon's circumference is 10,895 km/6,755 miles). The continent of Asia, of which China forms a large part, can easily cover the moon.

Which is the biggest island?

There are several different types of islands and lakes and the history of how they were formed also differs quite considerably. Islands are always surrounded by water, which can be either fresh or salt. Australia is sometimes described as an island, but, strictly speaking, this is wrong because it is a continent, and a continent cannot be described as an island.

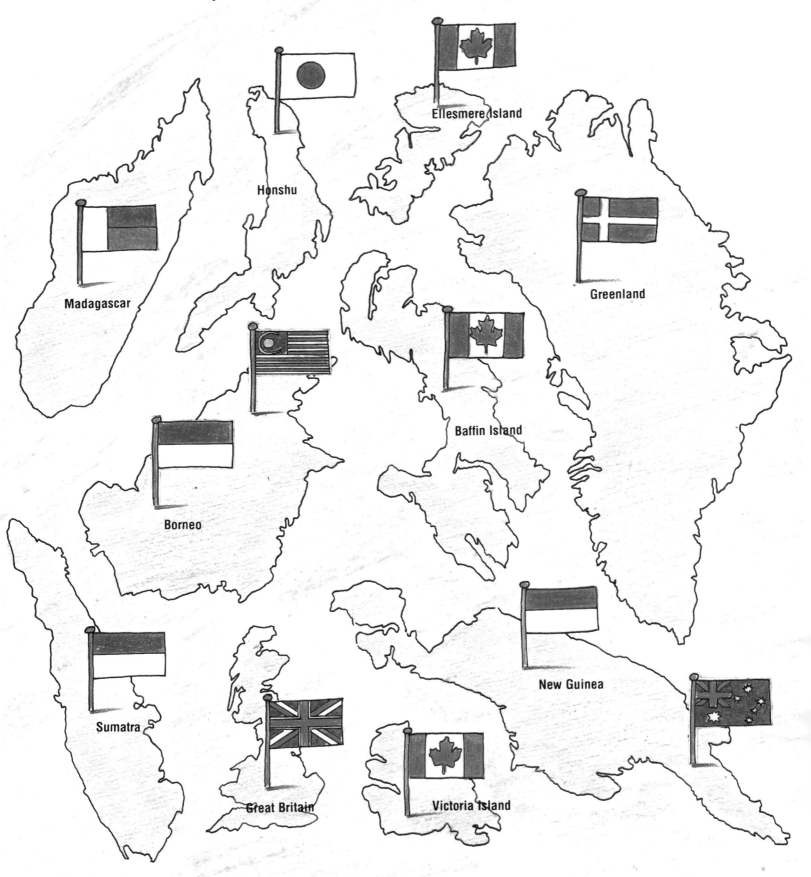

Honshu

Ellesmere Island

Madagascar

Greenland

Baffin Island

Borneo

Sumatra

New Guinea

Great Britain

Victoria Island

Some islands used to be part of the mainland and were separated by floods, violent storms or earth movements. Some islands were formed when volcanoes erupted or from coral reefs (atolls). Peninsulas are still connected to the mainland. Isles are separated from the mainland but lie close to it. Holms are small islands which are normally situated at the mouth of a river or very close to the mainland. Holms are also known as islets.

Greenland is the world's largest island. It was named by its discoverer, the Icelandic Eric the Red, because of the trees and green grass growing to the south of the island. Only about 16 per cent of the island is free of ice, however. The total area of Greenland is 2,176,000 km²/840,186 miles² and the island is situated in the North Atlantic Ocean. Although Greenland is connected to the American continent under water, it belongs to Denmark.

New Guinea (second largest island). New Guinea lies in the western Pacific Ocean, north of Australia, and covers an area of about 825,951 km²/318,900 miles². It is divided into Papua New Guinea and Irian Jaya, which is part of Indonesia.

Borneo (third largest island). Borneo lies in the Indian Ocean and belongs partly to Indonesia and partly to Malaysia. It is about 725,545 km²/282,962 miles² in area.

Madagascar (fourth). 590,000 km²/230,100 miles², in the Indian Ocean.

Baffin Island (fifth). 476,065 km²/185,665 miles², in the North Atlantic Ocean. It belongs to Canada.

Sumatra (sixth). 437,600 km²/170,664 miles², in the Indian Ocean. It belongs to Indonesia.

Honshu (seventh). 230,782 km²/89,105 miles². Honshu lies between the Pacific Ocean and the Sea of Japan, and is the largest of Japan's four main islands.

Great Britain (eighth). 218,041 km²/85,036 miles², in the North Atlantic. It is the main island of the United Kingdom.

Victoria Island (ninth). 212,197 km²/82,757 miles², in the North Atlantic. Part of Canada.

Ellesmere Island (tenth). 196,236 km²/76,532 miles², in the North Atlantic Ocean. Also part of Canada.

Lakes are not directly connected to the sea as they are entirely surrounded by land. Some lakes are the result of enormous ice, rock and rubble masses which shifted during the Ice Age. Glacial lakes of this kind are found in England, Europe and British Columbia in North America. Some lakes were formed by earth movements; entire sections of land were torn apart and lakes like the Dead Sea evolved. Other lakes are water-filled old volcanoes. Lakes of volcanic origin are found in Germany, Iceland, Italy and New Zealand.

The greatest lakes on earth			
Lake	(area in km²/ miles²)	max. depth in m/ft	length in km/miles
Caspian Sea (USSR and Iran)	360,700/139,000	980/3234	1225/766
Lake Superior (USA and Canada)	82,350/31,787	406/1340	560/356
Lake Victoria (Uganda, Tanzania, Kenya)	69,500/26,827	80/264	360/225
Aral Sea (USSR)	65,000/25,090	68/224	450/281
Lake Huron (USA and Canada)	59,600/23,005	228/752	330/206
Lake Michigan (USA)	58,000/22,388	281/927	494/309
Lake Tanganyika (Zaire, Tanzania, Zambia, Burundi)	32,900/12,699	1435/4735	725/453
Great Bear Lake (Canada)	31,800/12,275	82/271	373/233
Lake Baikal (USSR)	30,500/11,773	1940/6402	620/387
Lake Malawi (Tanzania, Malawi, Mozambique)	29,600/11,426	678/2237	580/362

Compared to this list, the largest lake in the United Kingdom, for instance, seems minute. Lough Neagh in Northern Ireland lies 14.6 meters/48 feet above sea level, is 29 km/18 miles long, 17.7 km/11 miles wide and has an area of 381.7 km²/147.4 miles. This lake would fit into the Caspian Sea 984 times! Compared to these islands, you would need a magnifying glass to see the island of Fehmarn (1851 km²/714 miles²) in the Baltic Sea.

The largest salt water lake is the Caspian Sea. Its water mass could flood the entire British Isles. Great Britain has a total area of around 218,000 km²/85,000 miles² and the Caspian Sea has an area of 360,700 km²/139,000 miles./².

Warm or cold-blooded?

Not all mammals have the same body temperature as human beings. Cold-blooded animals adjust their body temperature according to the temperature of their surroundings. The cold-blooded animals include fish, newts, reptiles and invertebrates. All other animals are warm-blooded, so are human beings. Warm-blooded animals keep their body temperature constant and do not rely on the temperature of their surroundings. They are specially protected against fluctuations in temperature by a dense covering of hair or feathers and a certain type of body grease. People are not protected in this way. They need clothing and shelter to protect them from the cold and from extreme heat.

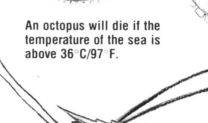

An octopus will die if the temperature of the sea is above 36°C/97°F.

Do people always have the same body temperature? When people are sick, their temperature often rises and they are said to run a fever. No human being can survive a body temperature of over 43°C/ 109°F. But too low a temperature can be dangerous, too. The circulation stops at temperatures below 36°C/97°F, and body temperatures below 20°C/68°F lead to death. The various body temperatures of humans are graded into certain categories:

36°C/97°F and below: collapse temperature
36°–37°C/97°–98.6°F: normal temperature
37.1°–38°C/99°–100.4°F: pre-febrile, i.e. pre-fever temperature
38.1°–38.5°C/10.6°–101.3°F: slight temperature (fever)
38.6°–39°C/101.5°–102.2°F: considerable temperature (fever)
39.1°–40.5°C/102.4–105°F: high temperature (fever)
above 40.5°C/105°F: very high temperature (fever)

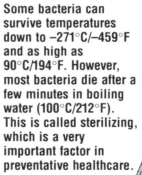

There is actually no need to boil shrimps as they cannot survive water temperatures over 26°C/78°F for long.

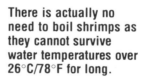

Some bacteria can survive temperatures down to −271°C/−459°F and as high as 90°C/194°F. However, most bacteria die after a few minutes in boiling water (100°C/212°F). This is called sterilizing, which is a very important factor in preventative healthcare.

An edible snail can survive temperatures of −100°C/148°F. It will die at 50°C/122°F, however.

The body temperature of a cat can drop down to 16°C/60°F when it will become unconscious, but can be revived.

A frog can be frozen at temperatures of −10°C/14°F and still survive.

104

Body temperature

The temperatures animals can survive at cannot easily be defined as it would be cruel to animals to make tests of this kind. The upper and lower temperature ranges have been discovered for some animals, however, and we know what temperature extremes some other creatures can survive.

The body temperature of domestic animals (in °C/°F)

Pigeon	41–43°/105–109°
Duck	41–43°/105–109°
Chicken	40.5–42°/104–107°
Goose	40–41°/104–105°
Goat	38.5–40.5°/101–104°
Sheep	38–40°/100–104°
Pig	38–40°/100–104°
Rabbit	37.5–39.5°/99–103°
Cat	38–39.5°/100–103°
Cow	37.5–39.5°/99–103°
Dog	37.5–39°/99–102°
Horse	37.5–39.5°/99–103°
House mouse	35.2–37.9°/95–100°

The body temperature of other warm-blooded animals (in °C/°F)

Anteater	23°/73°
Sloth	33°/91°
Whale	35.5°/95°
Elephant	36.4°/67°
Polar bear	37°/98°
Chimpanzee	37°/98°
Penguin	37.7°/70°
Rat	32.1–38.1°/60–70.5°
Wren	42–44°/107–111°
Ostrich	39.2°/102°
Owl	40.2°/104°
Sparrow	39.9–43.5°/104–110°

Can a cold-blooded animal also be warm-blooded? The answer is 'yes' because some horses are known as cold-blooded and others are warm-blooded. In fact, all horses are strictly warm-blooded, like other animals. Some heavy breeds of horses, such as the English Shire and the Belgian horse, are still called cold-blooded although their body temperature, like that of all horses, is between 37.5° and 39.5°C/ 99° and 103°F. Warm-blooded breeds are the English Thorough-bred, Arabian and the German Holstein horses.

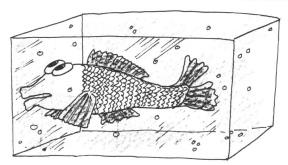

Fish sometimes get locked in the ice when a lake freezes over, but they can continue to swim at temperatures of −8° to −15°C/18° to 5°F once they have thawed out again. They die at temperatures of −20°C/ −4°F, however.

Is it possible to share your warm bath with a goldfish? Being cold-blooded, fish can adapt to the temperature of their surroundings and can tolerate temperatures between −20°C/−4°F and 38°C/100.4°F. The goldfish with an average body temperature of 23°C/73°F would probably die if you took it into a 40°C/104°F bath with you. Your dog would thoroughly enjoy a bath at that temperature, though he might object to the bubbles!

Is the sun the largest planet?

The volume of a body is called its cubic capacity. A sphere obviously has a different cubic capacity from a cube or a pyramid. The volume of a body is given in cubic measures, e.g. cubic meters (m³), cubic feet, liters or pints or gallons.

A liter, which is approximately 2.1 US pints, is equivalent to one-thousandth of a cubic meter (m³):

$$1 \text{ liter} = \frac{1}{1000} \text{ m}^3$$

To work out the volume of wood, the special measuring unit of a cubic meter of solid timber is used. This is calculated by the length and the diameter of the tree trunk. It gets even more complicated when the volume of stacked wood is called for. Here the cubic meter for stacked timber is used so that the space between the layers and stacks can be taken into account.

Calculating the volume

of various bodies differs according to their shape. The formuli for calculating the volume of some shapes are given below.

sphere

$$\frac{4}{3} \pi \cdot r^3$$

cylinder

$$\pi \, r^2 \cdot h$$

pyramid
(triangular base)

$$\frac{1}{3} l \, b \cdot h$$

cone

$$\frac{1}{3} \left(\frac{1}{2} a \cdot h_a \right) \cdot h = \frac{1}{6} a \cdot h_a \, h$$

cube

$$l \cdot b \cdot h$$

Explanation of symbols
π = 3.1459 . . .
l = length
h = height
r = radius = half the diameter
b = breadth

Can the volume of the earth be calculated? One way would be to use the formula for a sphere. The only snag is that the earth isn't a perfect sphere, in which the diameter from the center is always the same. The earth has quite a few dimples, ridges and dips, which makes the calculation of the volume quite difficult. It is therefore only possible to estimate its volume as being about 1,083,207,000,000 km³ or 2,548,705,800 miles³. The volume of the moon is about 21,900,000,000 km³ or 5,152,941,100 miles³, so you would need 49.5 times the volume of the moon to fill the volume of the earth. Calculating the volume of the other planets is even more difficult because they have not been explored and most of them are bigger than the earth, so it is only possible to work out approximate volumes. Here is an example for comparison. If the sun was a ball with a diameter of 30 cm or 1 foot, as pictured on the right, the earth would be the size of a pea, as would Venus. Uranus and Neptune would have the volume of a plum, Saturn that of a mandarin orange, and Jupiter that of an apple. Mars would be as small as a blackcurrant and Mercury the size of a mustard seed. Although the moon is not a planet, if you include it in this comparison compared to a fruit in relation to the sun it would also be the size of a mustard seed.

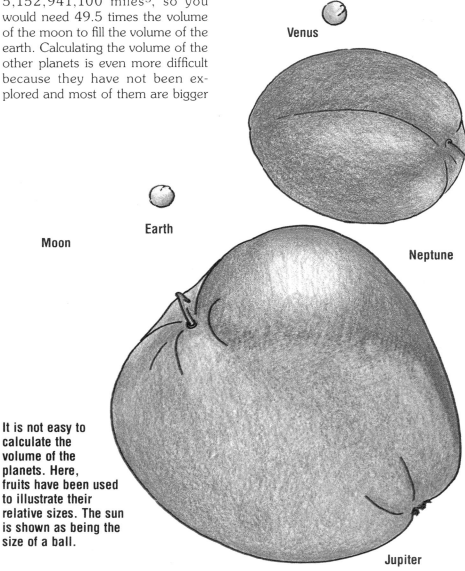

Venus

Earth

Moon

Neptune

It is not easy to calculate the volume of the planets. Here, fruits have been used to illustrate their relative sizes. The sun is shown as being the size of a ball.

Jupiter

Volume

Reservoirs which hold immense amounts of water also have a volume, but they have to supply thousands of people. It is essential to know the amount of water remaining in a reservoir so that a regular supply can be maintained. So the volume has to be calculated. It is quite difficult to work out the exact volume of large lakes or oceans because of various coastal features and water depths. The volumes of some lakes have been calculated, however. The Caspian Sea holds 89,600 km^3/21,083 miles^3 of salt water, almost four times as much as Lake Baikal, which holds 23,000 km^3/5,412 miles of fresh water. The volume of the Mediterranean sea, (4.38 million km^3/1.03 million miles^3) is 87 times greater than that of the North Sea (0.05 million km^3/11,765 million miles^3).

Reservoirs do not only serve as drinking water storage. They are also very important in the production of energy and the regulation of the water level of rivers, especially those used by ships. Very high and very low water levels are not satisfactory for shipping.

Distribution of water	per cent
Oceans and seas	97.29
Glaciers and ice caps	2.09
Underground rock or soil	0.6054
Rivers and Lakes	0.0144
Atmosphere	0.00094
Biosphere	0.00004

Sun

Of course the sun isn't really the size of a ball but this size is useful when comparing the various planets.

How much water can an oil

The largest oil tanker in the world, the *Seawise Giant*, measures 458 meters/1511 feet long by 63 meters/208 feet wide and can hold a load of 564,763 deadweight tonnes. That is an incredible amount. Swimming pools for international competitions have a length of 50 meters/165 feet, a width of 21 meters/69 feet and a depth of 2 meters/6½ feet. On this basis you could fit nine swimming pools lengthwise and three pools widthwise on to the largest tanker in the world. But even a giant like this can only take comparatively small amounts of water compared with a lake.

How do you know how much cargo a ship can hold? There are various ways of calculating the weight of a ship and its loading capacity. The internationally used system is the gross register ton (grt), net register ton (nrt), displacement tonnage and deadweight ton (tdw). Gross register tons are mainly used in commercial shipping. To calculate the amount of gross register tons the entire interior space of the ship is taken into account. One gross register ton equals 100 cubic feet/2.83 m³. The net register ton is the size of the hold of the ship, whether it is for cargo or passengers. It is calculated by taking the gross register tonnage and deducting the crew, engine and storage quarters. The displacement tonnage gives the total weight of a ship and its cargo. This is calculated by the amount of water the ship displaces. This unit is primarily used by the Navy. The load capacity of a ship is given in deadweight tons. That is the maximum weight the ship can take and includes the passengers, water, fuel, and provisions as well as the cargo. The deadweight tonnage is given in long tons, a unit generally used in navigation. 1 long ton = 2240 pounds = 1015 kg.

Around **100 years ago the tankers** were really tiny compared with the modern giants. The table on the right shows the size of some famous tankers of the past and how much cargo they could carry.

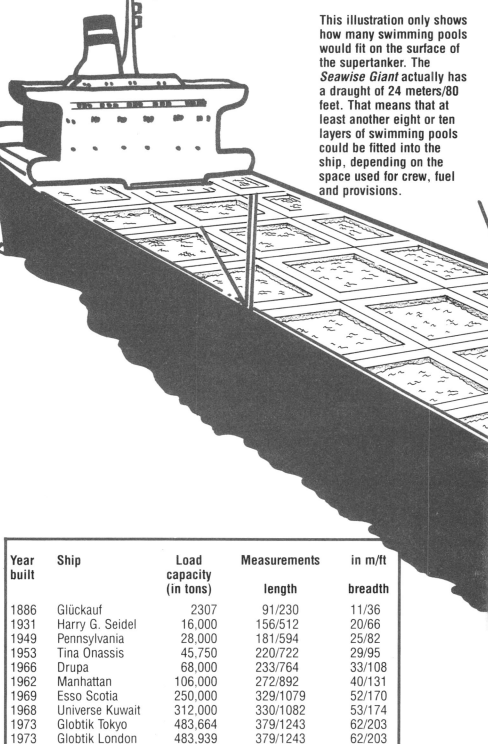

This illustration only shows how many swimming pools would fit on the surface of the supertanker. The *Seawise Giant* actually has a draught of 24 meters/80 feet. That means that at least another eight or ten layers of swimming pools could be fitted into the ship, depending on the space used for crew, fuel and provisions.

Year built	Ship	Load capacity (in tons)	Measurements in m/ft length	breadth
1886	Glückauf	2307	91/230	11/36
1931	Harry G. Seidel	16,000	156/512	20/66
1949	Pennsylvania	28,000	181/594	25/82
1953	Tina Onassis	45,750	220/722	29/95
1966	Drupa	68,000	233/764	33/108
1962	Manhattan	106,000	272/892	40/131
1969	Esso Scotia	250,000	329/1079	52/170
1968	Universe Kuwait	312,000	330/1082	53/174
1973	Globtik Tokyo	483,664	379/1243	62/203
1973	Globtik London	483,939	379/1243	62/203
1976	Batillus	550,698	414/1358	63/207

tanker hold?

The largest oil tank in the world holds a total of 238,158,000 liters/5,292,400 gallons. Five tanks of this size are situated in the Saudi Arabian oil-producing area of Ju'aymah. They are each 22 meters/73 feet high and have a diameter of 117 meters/386 feet. The gasoline tanks that lie underneath a gas station are comparatively small: they only hold about 20,000 liters/4500 gallons. And the oil tank of a family house holds a maximum of about 5000 liters/1100 gallons.

The largest building on earth, judging by its volume, is a hangar belonging to the plane-building company Boeing in Everett, USA. It has a volume of 5.6 million m³/198 million cubic feet. If you wanted to fill this hangar with water from a waterfall it would take several minutes and in some cases hours.

Waterfalls	
Boyoma Waterfall	5 min 29 s
Guaira Waterfall	1 min 10 s
Khone Waterfall	8 min 7 s
Niagara Falls	15 min 36 s
Paolo Afonso	33 min 20 s
Urubupunga	54 min 34 s
Iguaçu	54 min 54 s
Victoria Falls	1 h 24 min 28 s
Rhine (Switzerland)	2 h 13 min

The greatest waterfalls (by discharge volume)

	average discharge
Boyoma (Zaire)	17,000 m³/s / 600,270 ft³/s
Guaira (Brazil/Uruguay)	13,000 m³/s / 459,030 ft³/s
Khone (Mekong/Laos)	11–12,000 m³/s / 388,410–423,720 ft³/s
Niagara Falls (USA/Canada)	6000 m³/s / 211,860 ft³/s
Paolo Afonso (Brazil)	2800 m³/s / 98,868 ft³/s
Urubupunga (Brazil)	2700 m³/s / 95,337 ft³/s
Iguaçu (Brazil/Argentina)	1700 m³/s / 60,027 ft³/s
Victoria (Zambia/Zimbabwe)	1100 m³/s / 38,841 ft³/s
Rhine (Switzerland)	700 m³/s / 24,717 ft³/s

What is a veil? The answer to that question is not as simple as it appears. Apart from the veil worn by a woman at her wedding or for cultural reasons, there is also a veil of water. Although some waterfalls are very high they carry so little water that it breaks up into a fine mist as the water drops. The result is a 'veil' of water mist.

The largest tankers

Name	tdw	grt	breadth m	ft	length m	ft
Seawise Giant (Liberia)	564,763	238,558	63	208	458	1511
Pierre Guillaumat (France)	555,051	274,838	62	205	414	1366
Batillus (France)	553,662	273,550	62	205	413	1363
Esso Atlantic (Liberia)	516,893	234,638	71	234	406	1340
Nanny (Sweden)	491,120	245,140	78	257	363	1198
Nissei Maru (Japan)	484,337	238,517	61	202	378	1247
Globtik London (Liberia)	483,933	213,894	61	202	378	1247
Burmah Enterprise (UK)	457,927	231,629	68	224	378	1247
Burmah Endeavour (UK)	457,841	231,629	67	221	278	1247

Compared with this giant, a sailing yacht is tiny. But at 15 meters/50 feet long it is still as long as two cars parked one behind the other.

109

Who uses the most energy?

During many millions of years several natural sources of energy have been formed on earth – coal, oil, natural gas, and radioactive uranium. The sun and the power of water are also natural energy sources. All these types of energy are called 'primary energy' from which 'secondary energy', such as electrical power and petrol, is produced. Scientists have worked out how much energy per head is used on earth. The energy consumption of a country depends on the number of factories in the land, whether many electricity-gobbling appliances are used in the households, and whether the climate calls for a lot of heating.

The consumption of primary energy is calculated by the heat generated by 1 tonne (t) of coal (1 tonne coal equivalent = 1 t C.E.), which has a heat volume of 29,400,000 kilojoules (kJ).

On average, one person uses around 145,000 kJ of energy daily, which is about 5 kg C.E.

Ninety per cent of the energy required by all factories, transport vehicles and machinery on earth is produced from 'fossil' energy sources like coal, oil and natural gas. One hundred years ago, energy was mainly produced from coal and wood. Horses and oxen were used instead of cars, tractors and lorries. Some poorer and less developed countries still do so today.

North America and Western Europe together use 4.1 billion t C.E. That is 45 per cent of the total energy produced annually on earth (9.2 billion t C.E.). There are a total of 708 million people living in North America and Western Europe, whereas a total of 855 million people live in Africa and South America. But the industrial countries still use at least six times more energy than the developing countries.

Another unit used to measure consumption apart from the coal equivalent is the unit of oil. In very poor but also very warm countries like Ethiopia, only about 23 kg/50 lb units of oil per head are used in a year. One person from Western Europe or North America uses nearly 190 times as much energy as a person from Ethiopia.

In very poor countries people often only have just enough fuel to cook and keep themselves warm. When they need more fuel they have to clear great areas of woodland which greatly damages the environment.

The production of energy causes great problems for the environment, especially in highly developed countries. Many people who are concerned about the environment are therefore demanding that more gentle sources, such as the energy of the sun or the wind,

In many very poor countries, animal dung and fire wood are often the only sources of energy that people can afford, because they do not need expensive processing. Rich countries can buy 'energy' in the form of oil and gas. For this reason, people in these richer countries can use a great number of electrical appliances in their homes.

or the gas produced by garbage and manure, should be used instead. Energy generated by water and fire-wood is used only rarely in industrial countries – about 2 per cent of the total energy consumption. Mineral oil provides the greatest source of energy – about 42 per cent. In addition, there is the energy produced by coal (22 per cent), gas (16 per cent), brown coal (10 per cent), and nu-

clear energy (8 per cent).

People living in warmer countries have an advantage because they don't need to heat their homes as much as people in colder countries. In cooler countries, heating the house uses up 80 per cent of a household's energy consumption. The rest is gobbled up by domestic appliances (17 per cent) and lighting (3 per cent).

Washing dishes by hand not only saves energy but water, too.

The power consumption of domestic appliances and 'economy' appliances
(in kilowatts)

refrigerator	0.6–0.8 kW
(per 100 liters/22 gals/24 hrs)	
freezer	0.4–0.6 kW
(per 100 liters/22 gals/24 hrs)	
economy refrigerator	0.2 kW
(per 100 liters/22 gals/24 hrs)	
washing machine	0.5–0.8 kW
(hot cycle/per 1 kg/2.2 lb dry clothing)	
economy washing machine	0.4 kW
(30% less water)	
dishwasher	1.5–2.0 kW
(hot cycle at 60°C)	
economy dishwasher	0.9 kW
(60% less water)	

How much energy (kg oil units per person) is used where?

	1960	1981
Nepal	3	10
Mali	10	21
Ethiopia	7	23
Kenya	114	147
Ecuador	151	571
Brazil	264	740
Spain	667	1902
Italy	1003	2558
Japan	80	3087
USSR	2029	4736
USA	5863	7540

Energy is the capacity for doing work. Sources of energy are coal, oil and natural gas, water and wind power and the rays of the sun. These are usually converted into other forms of energy which we can use – electrical, mechanical and chemical energy, heat and radiation energy. The water power of a reservoir, for instance, drives gigantic turbines which in turn produce electrical energy. The physical measuring unit for energy, work and heat is Joule (J). When energy is converted into work it is measured in Watts (W).

One joule of energy used in one second is the equivalent of one Watt (1 W = 1J/s). Every day each person uses an average of 532,000 kJ (1 kilojoule = 1000 Joule) of energy (from oil, coal and so on). That is about 16.5 kg/36 lb of coal per day. This coal could produce around 148 kilowatt hours (kWh) of power in a power station. That amount of power would wash over 211 kg/464 lb of washing in a washing machine.

Oil, natural gas and coal are 'fossil' fuels. They have taken millions of years to form. Oil and gas are formed from decomposed micro-organisms deep in the ground. Coal originates from plant matter. In prehistoric times huge

# of energy?

With one flick of its wing a honey bee converts the energy of 0.0008 Joule. The chirping of a cricket is the equivalent of 0.0004 Joule.

A burning match generates 4 kilojoules of energy. If you could use the energy of 600 burning matches to generate power, you would get 0.7 kilowatt hours, enough to wash 1 kg/2.2 lb of washing in a washing machine.

Each person uses around 532,000 kilojoules of energy every day. The source of that energy would be 16.5 kg/36 lb bricks of compressed coal, for example.

forests of trees died and created enormous bogs. New layers of soil were deposited on top of these and the dead trees were cut off from the air supply. As more and more layers of earth pressed down on them, they gradually turned into brown and black coal.

The amount of fossil fuels available on earth will supply us with energy for a few more centuries. But supplies are limited even if the reserves are still great. Scientists estimate that there are reserves of oil on earth of nearly 86.8 trillion tonnes (= 86,800,000,000 t). Even greater are the reserves of coal: 15 trillion tonnes (= 15,000,000,000,000 t).

One Horsepower (HP) is the equivalent of 0.745 kW. One Hp is the power to lift 1 kg/2.2 lb 1 meter/3 feet in one second. The engine of a small car has about 74 horsepower, i.e. it would take 74 horses to pull the car with the same power as the engine can drive it. A horse can only provide 1 HP or 0.745 kW over a short time, however. The sustained power output of a horse is actually 0.4 kW. Therefore you would in fact need 137 horses to provide the same power as a car. The maximum power output of a human being is about 0.7 kW, but sustained work only yields 0.1 kW.

Various power output figures:	
(1000 Watt = 1 kilowatt; 1 megawatt = 1000 kW)	
human heart	0.0004 kW
human being (sustained)	0.1 kW
human being (short-term)	0.7 kW
horse (sustained)	0.4 kW
horse (short-term)	0.745 kW
railway engine	5 MW
solar power station	max. 10 MW
tidal power station (annual maximum)	544,000 MW
nuclear power station (Biblis A+B)	2386 MW
largest power station in the world (Grand Coulee, USA)	10.080 MW
radiation of the sun	approx. 4×10^{20} MW

To achieve the same power output as a car (74 HP) one would need to harness 137 horses to a carriage because one horsepower isn't necessarily the same as the power of one horse.

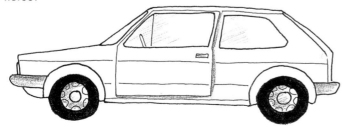

The greatest source of energy is the sun. Every day we receive 10.000 times more energy than the entire earth population needs. Unlike fossil fuels, this source of energy is almost inexhaustible.

How heavy is flyweight?

A fly, such as the common house fly, weighs less than 1 g – 0.013 g to be exact. In contrast, a flyweight in weight lifting weighs up to 52 kg/114 lb, or 400,000 times as much. The flyweight is the lightest category in weight lifting. Many types of sport have different weight categories. This means that only opponents of approximately the same weight may face each other in a contest. Weights are also of great importance in other types of sport. The balls used in many games must always be of the correct weight.

Weight categories vary from sport to sport. If a sportsman weighing 65 kg/145 lb wanted to take part in wrestling, boxing, weight lifting and judo, he would be a half-lightweight for judo, a lightweight for weight lifting and wrestling, and a welterweight for boxing, all at the same time. If that sportsman also wanted to try hammer throwing, stone throwing or weight throwing, he would be a featherweight, too.

Weight categories in sport:

Weight lifting	kg/lb
flyweight	under 52/114.5
bantamweight	under 56/123.5
featherweight	under 60/132.5
lightweight	under 67.5/149
middleweight	under 75/165.5
light heavyweight	under 82.5/182
middle heavyweight	under 90/198.5
first heavyweight	under 100/220.5
second heavyweight	under 110/242.5
super heavyweight	above 110/242.5

Boxing (Amateurs)	kg/lb
half flyweight	under 48/105.5
flyweight	under 51/112
bantamweight	under 54/118
featherweight	under 57/126
lightweight	under 60/135
half welterweight	under 63.5/140
welterweight	under 67/147
half middleweight	under 71/155
middleweight	under 75/158
light heavyweight	under 91/175
heavyweight	above 91/175

Wrestling	kg/lb
paperweight	under 48/105.5
flyweight	under 52/114.5
bantamweight	under 57/126
featherweight	under 62/136
lightweight	under 68/150
welterweight	under 74/163
middleweight	under 82/180
light heavyweight	under 90/198.5
heavyweight	under 100/220.5
super heavyweight	above 100/220.5

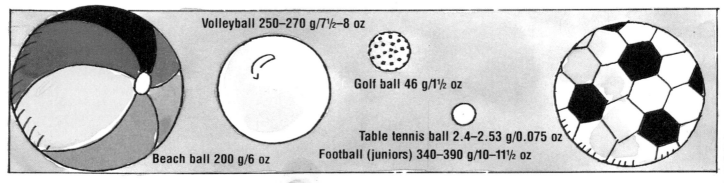

Volleyball 250–270 g/7½–8 oz

Golf ball 46 g/1½ oz

Table tennis ball 2.4–2.53 g/0.075 oz

Football (juniors) 340–390 g/10–11½ oz

Beach ball 200 g/6 oz

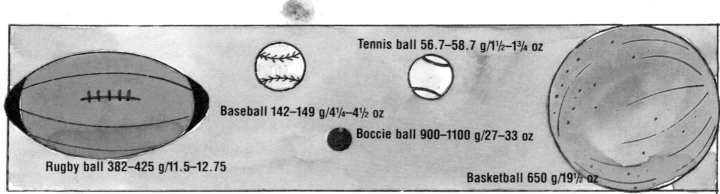

Tennis ball 56.7–58.7 g/1½–1¾ oz

Baseball 142–149 g/4¼–4½ oz

Boccie ball 900–1100 g/27–33 oz

Rugby ball 382–425 g/11.5–12.75

Basketball 650 g/19½ oz

The list on the right shows the number of table tennis balls you would need to equal the weight of the balls used in various games.

Number of table tennis balls			
Beach ball	80	Tennis ball	23
Volleyball	104	Baseball	59
Golf ball	18	Medicine ball	2000
Football (soccer)	146	Boccie ball	440
Rugby ball	160	Basketball	260
		(average weights)	

Weight

Judo	Men kg/lb	Women kg/lb
super lightweight	under 60/132	under 48/105.5
half lightweight	under 65/136	under 52/114
light weight	under 71/156	under 56/123
half middleweight	under 78/171.5	under 61/134
middleweight	under 86/189	under 66/145
half heavyweight	under 95/210	under 72/158
heavyweight	above 95/210	above 72/158

This muscleman must be a heavyweight – or even a super heavyweight?

Heavy athletics (hammer throwing etc.)	kg/lb
featherweight	under 65/136
lightweight	under 70/154
middleweight	under 75/165
light heavyweight	under 82.5/182
middle heavyweight	under 90/198.5
heavyweight	above 90/198.5

A London bus is the same weight as 5 elephants.
A tractor weighs the same as 2 elephants. How do other heavy vehicles compare?

	weight tonnes	number of elephants
tractor	7.4	about 2
coach	12	3
London bus	20	5
omnibus	16	4
shovel dredger	14.9	about 3½
lorry/truck (loaded)	40	10
large lorry (unloaded)	12–15	3
truck in USA (loaded)	44	11

These two vehicles, a London bus and a tractor, together weigh the same as 7 elephants.

It is much easier to move forward on land than it is in the water – almost twice as easy, to be exact. The reason is that the resistance of water is higher than that of a smooth road, so much more effort or power is needed to achieve the same result in water as on land. Thanks to better engines and improved ships' hulls which can cut through the water, however, modern ships can go four times as fast as the ships of one hundred years ago.

How are speeds measured on the water? It is quite complicated to calculate accurately the speed at which a person or animal moves through the water. The calculation should include the distance, the time needed to cover the distance, the type of current, the wind conditions, and so on. Measuring the speed of animals in the water is even more difficult than measuring the speed of people. They are often faster when they feel threatened and it is not easy to check whether they can maintain their speed over longer distances. The figures given in the table below are therefore only assumed maximum speeds. Measuring the speed of ships is a different matter, however. For over 150 years the best motor-powered ships have competed to win the Blue Riband for the fastest crossing of the Atlantic. As all the ships have to travel more or less the same distance, the average speed can be calculated quite accurately.

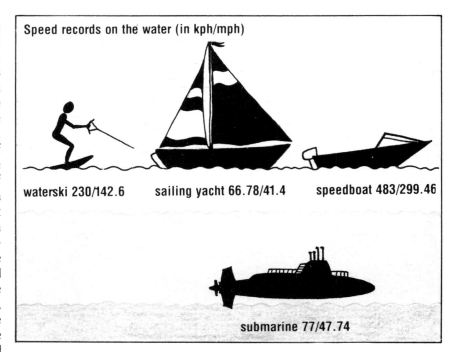

Speed records on the water (in kph/mph)

waterski 230/142.6   sailing yacht 66.78/41.4   speedboat 483/299.46

submarine 77/47.74

100 years ago motor boats were almost as fast as a blue whale. In 1889 the *City of Paris*, a twin-screw steamer, won the Blue Riband for the fastest Atlantic crossing. Her speed was about 37 kph/22.9 mph, the same as that of a blue whale. Modern ships are considerably faster.

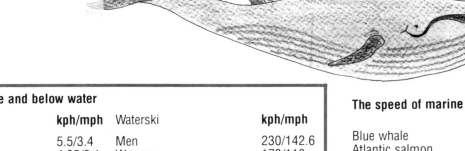

Top speeds above and below water

Swimming	kph/mph	Waterski	kph/mph
Men	5.5/3.4	Men	230/142.6
Women	4.95/3.1	Women	178/110
Rowing		World War II	
(single, Channel crossing)	9.8/6	submarine	32.4/20
Surfing		Modern submarine	77/47.7
(windspeed 7–9)	57/35	Small motorboat	253/157
Sailing (22 m/73 ft yacht)	66.87/41	Speedboat	483/299.46
Sailing ship		Motor ship (1860)	25/15.5
(commercial)	37/23	Passenger liner	
Sailing, catamaran	58/36	(*Queen Elizabeth II*)	52/32.2

The speed of marine creatures

	kph/mph
Blue whale	36.5/33.6
Atlantic salmon	37/22.9
Sealion	40/24.8
Dolphin	44.4/27.5
Dwarf whale	46/28.5
Sword whale	55.5/34.4
Tunafish	69.8/43.3
Yellowfin tuna	75/46.5
Fanfish	109/67.5

The Blue Riband for the fastest Atlantic crossing

The Blue Riband is awarded for the fastest crossing of the Atlantic between Bishop's Rock (in the south-west corner of England) and the Ambrose light vessel just off the coast from New York (USA), a distance of exactly 2958 nautical miles (5441 km). A ship must break the previous speed record for this crossing to win the Blue Riband. The largest and most modern ships have competed to win this prestigious award and a cup, the 'North Atlantic Blue Riband Challenge Trophy'. The ship winning the trophy may keep it until the record is broken by another ship. Some ships have won the Blue Riband several times. Since 1952 the Blue Riband has been held by the *United States*, a four-screw passenger liner (53,329 grt), and her record is still unbroken. The *United States* made the crossing in just three days, 10 hours and 40 minutes, with an average speed of 35.59 knots per hour (66 kph). In 1838 the Atlantic crossing took at least 15 days (with a speed of 8.8 knots or 16 kmh). At the turn of the century, reaching the other side of the 'big pond' still took nearly six days.

The winners of the Blue Riband (selection). Only ships that have held the trophy for at least three months are accepted on the official list of winners.			
Great Western (1838)	paddle wheels	8.8 kn	(16.2 kph)
Britannia (1840)	paddle wheels	10.6 kn	(19.6 kph)
City of Brussels (1869)	single screw	14.7 kn	(27 kph)
Servia (1881)	single screw	16 kn	(29.6 kph)
Oregon (1884) (2×)	single screw	18.2 kn	(33.7 kph)
City of Paris (1889) (2×)	twin screw	20 kn	(37 kph)
Luciana (1894)	twin screw	22 kn	(40.7 kph)
Mauretania (1907) (3×)	triple screw	23.7 kn	(44.4 kph)
Lusitania (1907) (3×)	triple screw	34 kn	(44.4 kph)
Bremen (1929) (2×)	4 screws	27.8 kn	(51 kph)
Queen Mary (1936) (2×)	4 screws	30.1 kn	(56 kph)
United States (1952)	4 screws	35.59 kn	(66 kph)

(The number of times the trophy was won in brackets)

Distances and speeds on the water

1 cable length = ¹/₁₀ nautical mile = 185.3 m, formerly used to measure anchor cables
1 nautical mile = 1.852 km/1.15 mile
1 knot = 1 nautical mile per hour
1 run = the distance a ship travels during 24 hours

How long will it take father and son to row across the lake? Well, the lake is calm, there is hardly any wind, even the duck can keep up with them!
Answer: They will probably need hours, days, or even weeks to move away from this spot. They are rowing in a circle! Never mind, practice makes perfect!

How long is a year?

It takes one day for the earth to turn once on its axis and one year for the earth to circle the sun. The reason for the seasons being so different in climate in countries away from the equator is that the earth does not orbit the sun in an upright position but at a slight angle. First the northern hemisphere receives more sunlight, then the southern hemisphere.

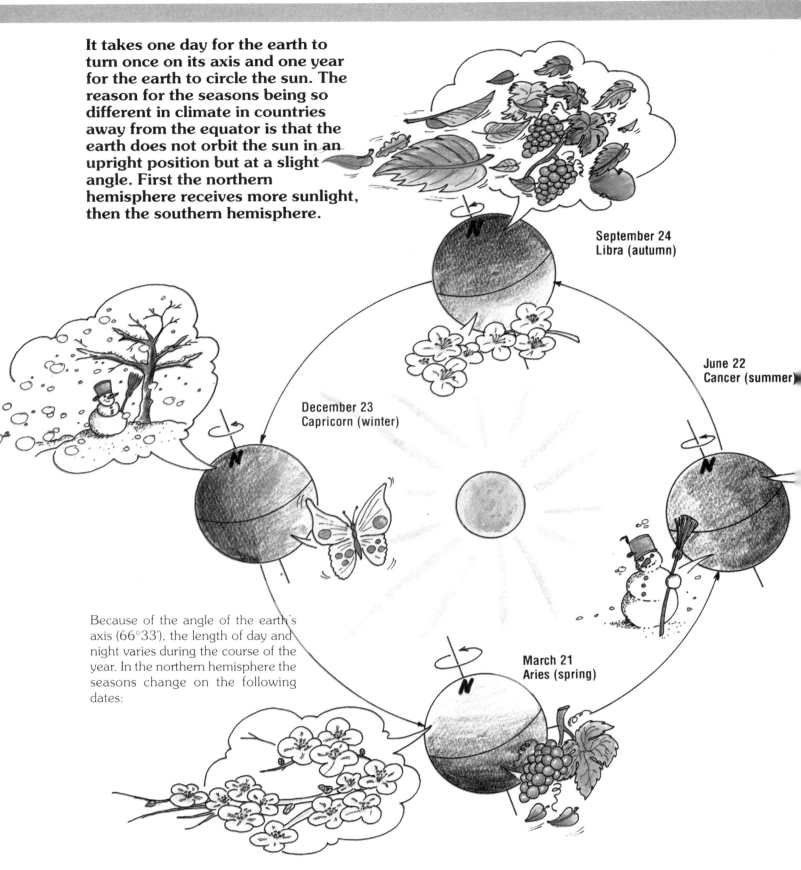

September 24 Libra (autumn)

June 22 Cancer (summer)

December 23 Capricorn (winter)

March 21 Aries (spring)

Because of the angle of the earth's axis (66°33'), the length of day and night varies during the course of the year. In the northern hemisphere the seasons change on the following dates:

March 21: First day of spring. Day and night are of equal length. On the southern hemisphere it is always the opposite.

June 22: First day of summer, the day of the summer solstice (the opposite is the winter solstice) when the sun has reached its highest point (the longest day).

September 24: First day of autumn. Both hemispheres are at the same distance from the sun. Day and night are the same length.

December 23: First day of winter (the shortest day).

The astronomical year has exactly 365.25636 mean solar days when the earth circles the sun at an average speed of 107 kph/66.3 mph (or 29.76 kph/18.45 miles per second). The earth's orbit measures a total of 936 million km (580 million miles).

Until the beginning of the 16th century people believed that the earth was the *centre of the universe*. In 1503, the astronomer Nicholas Copernicus (1473–1543) put forward the 'heliocentric' view of the world, in which the sun forms the centre of the universe. The sun only appears to wander through the signs of the zodiac. The latitudes of 23°27'F in the northern hemis-

phere is called the Tropic of Cancer. The same latitude in the southern hemisphere is called the Tropic of Capricorn. These are the points where the sun is at its zenith on June 22 and December 23 at 12 o'clock noon.

In astrology the signs of the zodiac represent the 12 'types' of human being because astrologers believe that the fortune of a person is governed by the position of the stars at his birth.

The signs of the zodiac. There are 12 signs of the zodiac. Six of them (Aries to Virgo) lie north of the celestial equator and the other six (Libra to Pisces) lie in the southern sky.

At the beginning of the four seasons the sun is in these signs: Aries (spring), Cancer (summer), Libra (autumn) and Capricorn (winter).

Astrologers believe that the constellation of the stars does not only influence our seasons but that all our earthly happenings depend on the stars, even the fortunes of human beings. According to astrology, the sign of the zodiac under which a person is born can reveal a great deal about his character.

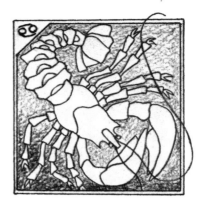

Sign for summer
Cancer (22.6–23.7)

Sign for spring
Aries (21.3–20.4)

Sign for autumn
Libra (24.9–23.10)

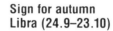

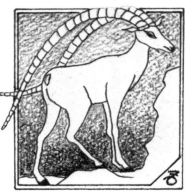

Sign for winter
Capricorn (23.12–20.1)

The signs of the zodiac	
Aries	March 21–April 20
Taurus	April 21–May 20
Gemini	May 21–June 21
Cancer	June 22–July 23
Leo	July 24–August 23
Virgo	August 24–September 23
Libra	September 24–October 23
Scorpio	October 24–November 22
Sagittarius	November 23–December 22
Capricorn	December 23–January 20
Aquarius	January 21–February 19
Pisces	February 20–March 20

The seasons				
Northern Hemisphere	**Astronomical Season**	**Meteorological Season**	**Southern Hemisphere**	**Zodiac Sign**
Spring	21.3.–22.5.	March–May	Autumn	Aries
Summer	22.6.–23.8.	June–August	Winter	Cancer
Autumn	24.0.–22.11.	Sept.–Nov.	Spring	Libra
Winter	23.12.–21.2.	Dec.–February	Summer	Capricorn

Which is the most accurate

Our ancestors wanted to know the time, but they didn't have watches and clocks. So they built sundials, water clocks or sand glasses. The sundial is an invention of the ancient Egyptians. The simplest type is a stick fixed into the ground or to a wall, so that the shadow of the stick moves with the sun. Sundials are not very accurate, however. They don't show the time in the dark and the sun's angle at which the sun shines on the stick varies with the seasons.

Waterclocks give the time at night as well as during the day. Water drips through the small opening of a container into another vessel and lifts a swimmer with an indicator. The walls of the vessel are marked with the hours. The waterclock and the sand glass (which works on the same principle as an egg timer) are both inaccurate because they cannot indicate minutes and seconds correctly. As time went by, people invented clocks which have continued to become smaller and more accurate.

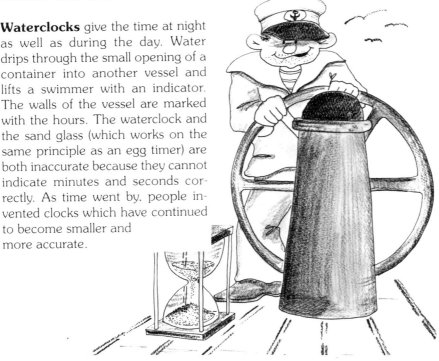

This sailor uses a sand glass to tell the time

Sea dogs keep different times from landlubbers. Even today the timekeeping on some ships is still the same as it was in the days of the sand glass. In a sand glass the sand takes exactly half an hour to run down from the top into the bottom, from the time a bell is struck. Eight bells indicate four hours and four hours makes up a watch. The watch begins at 08:00 hours. The ship's bell then strikes once at 08:30, twice at 09:00 hours, three times at 09:30 and so on. When the bell strikes eight times at noon the sailor knows it's time for food, so down to the galley!

The ancient Romans had a similar timekeeping system. The twelve hours of the night were divided into four night watches called vigils.

The day of mediaeval monks was extra long and started before sunrise. The time system of monks is called canonical hours. This word has nothing at all to do with cannons but means 'according to the standards of the church'. The canonical hours are divided into eight: Matins, Lauds, Prime, Terce, Sext, None, Vespers and Compline.

Matins was the night service, in the early morning hours between 02:30 and 03:00.

Lauds was the morning service between 05:00 and 06:00 hours, ending with daybreak.

Prime (the first hour) was shortly before sunrise, about 07:30 hours.

Terce (the third hour) was around 09:00 hours.

Sext (the sixth hour) which is twelve noon and also the time for lunch.

None (the ninth hour) was between 14:00 and 15:00 hours.

Vespers was the evening service around 16:30 hours at the beginning of dusk. It was customary in many abbeys to have supper just before darkness fell.

Compline was night prayers at around 18:00 hours. The monks had to be in their beds by 19:00 hours at the latest.

The time system of the monks was fairly inaccurate because sunrise and sundown are never at the same time on two consecutive days. Scientists have found that sunrise can be calculated with the help of longitudes (the earth is divided into 360 longitudes and 180 latitudes).

Sunrise differs by about four minutes per longitude and the times of sunrise and sundown also vary from day to day and month to month. This table shows how the times of sunrise and sundown vary throughout the year.

Month	Sunrise a.m.	Sundown p.m.
January	08:35–08:11	16:36–17:21
February	08:10–07:20	17:23–18:11
March	07:18–06:12	18:12–19:02
April	06:09–05:08	19:04–19:51
May	05:07–04:24	19:53–20:35
June	04:23–04:21	20:36–20:50
July	04:21–04:55	20:50–20:20
August	04:56–05:43	20:19–19:21
September	05:44–06:29	19:18–18:14
October	06:31–07:21	18:11–17:09
November	07:23–08:11	17:08–16:30
December	08:12–08:35	16:30–16:35

Which is the most accurate clock? Modern quartz watches are very accurate. They give the correct hours, minutes, seconds and even the right date over a period of several years. The only type of clock which is superior to the quartz clocks is the atomic clock.

An atomic clock is absolutely accurate over a period of 35,000 years. One of the world's most accurate atomic clocks is installed at the National Physical Laboratory at Teddington near London. This clock regulates all other public clocks at airports, railway stations and other public places. The atomic clock transmits the time via electronic signals to so-called mother clocks in all major cities. These mother clocks are connected to the public clocks, giving their signals minute by minute. That is the reason that the displays of public clocks move forward in small jerks every minute.

A modern watch is so small that it fits on every child's wrist. When they were first constructed, however, the complicated mechanics of watches needed quite a lot more space. The first watches were almost too large to fit into the pocket of a waistcoat. They were larger than an egg. The first pocket watch was made by a locksmith in Nuremberg. Germany.

Peter Henlein (1504). the inventor of the mainspring.

Even more accurate than accurate is a time-measuring instrument developed by German biochemists of the Max-Planck Institute near Munich – it measures time units of 2 billionths of a second. It is used to determine the time lapses in the smallest particles of the elements. atomic movements.

The largest single-faced clock in the world is the Colgate Clock in New Jersey (USA). Its dial has a diameter of 15.24 meters/50 feet. That is the height of 11 ten-year-olds standing on top of each other, but because they would be standing with their feet on the shoulders of the child below, 15 ten-year-olds would be needed to measure out the clock. The minute hand of this giant clock is as long as six ten-year-olds lying down (8.31 meters/27 ft 3 in). Compared to that, a wrist watch is absolutely minute.

Which is the biggest river in

When comparing the large rivers of the world the length of a river is usually the determining factor. But of the same importance are also the size of the area a river supplies with water (catchment basin) and the amount of water it carries.

The longest river on earth is the Nile in Africa. It is 6670 km/4145 miles long. The **largest** river is the Amazon in South America. At 6448 km/4007 miles long, it is 222 km/138 miles shorter than the Nile, but its catchment basin is almost twice as large. The basin of the Nile covers about 3.35 million km²/1.3 million miles², whereas the Amazon covers an area of almost 7.1 million km²/2.72 miles². It has about 15,000 tributaries, of which ten are more than 1600 km/1000 miles long. In comparison, the Rhine is only 1320 km/818 miles long. The mouth of the Amazon (320 km/198.4 miles) is so large that the distance between the banks of the river is the same as the distance from London to Paris.

The amount of water flowing per second (the 'mean discharge volume') is largest in the Amazon: 180,000 cubic metres or 6,354,000 cubic feet per second. That is over 110 times as much as the Nile.

Dams. The largest reservoir in the world is at Bratsk in the USSR which has a volume of 16,925,000 ha/m (137,214,000 acre/ft). The largest volume of water in the world is found at the dam of the Owen Falls in Uganda (Africa). This dam holds 246 billion cubic metres or 8.684 trillion cubic feet of water.

The Amazon isn't the longest river in the world but it is the largest. It holds the most water and has the largest catchment basin. Its giant mouth is as wide as the distance between London and Paris (320 km/198.4 miles).

Section of a map of Europe showing the distance between London and Paris.

London

Paris

Rivers

The highest dam on earth has a height of 325 metres/1072.5 feet and dams the river Vakhsh in the USSR.

Sunrise over the Amazon. To illustrate the size of its mouth London has been placed on one of its banks and Paris on the other. It is hard to imagine a river so wide, 320 km/198.4 miles, that you cannot see from one bank to the other.

Selected waterfalls

Name	Country	Total height (m/ft)
Angel Falls	Venezuela	979/3212
Tugela	South Africa	948/3128
Yosemite Falls	USA	739/2439
Takkakaw Falls	Canada	503/1660
Gavarnie Falls	France	421/1389
Krimmler Falls	Austria	380/1254
Skykkjedal Falls	Norway	330/990
Staubbach Falls	Switzerland	330/990
Gersoppa Falls	India	253/835
Eas-Coul-Aulin	UK	200/658
Triberg Falls	West Germany	163/538
Toce Falls	Italy	160/528
Akaka Falls	Hawaii	130/429
Victoria Falls	Zimbabwe	110/363
Powerscourt Falls	Ireland	106/350
Iguaçu Falls	Brazil/Argentina	82/271
Niagara Falls	Canada/USA	51/168

Selected rivers of the earth

Name	catchment basin (km²/miles²)
Amazon	7,050,000/2,722,000
Nile	3,350,000/1,293,000
Mississippi	3,221,000/1,244,000
Yangtze	1,959,000/756,000
Congo	3,457,000/1,293,000
Niger	1,890,000/730,000
Rio de la Plata-Parana	4,145,000/1,600,000
Volga	1,360,000/525,000
Zambezi	1,330,000/514,000
Rio Grande	445,000/172,000
Indus	1,166,000/450,000
Danube	816,000/315,000
Nelson	1,072,000/414,000
Rhine	160,000/62,000
Thames	10,000/4,000

How quickly does hair grow?	**Growth**	6
How do you transport 18 elephants?	**Space and aircraft**	8
Where does the sun shine most?	**Weather**	10
How fast do children grow?	**Body sizes**	12
What lives at the highest altitudes?	**Altitudes**	14
How many babies do mammals have?	**Reproduction**	16
Are birds the only creatures that lay eggs?	**Reproduction**	18
How quickly do mammals grow?	**Mammals**	20
How deep can deep-sea divers go?	**Deep-sea life**	22
Who lives the longest?	**Age**	24
Where does water boil at 71°C?	**Temperature**	26
Who can jump the furthest?	**Jumping**	28
Where are icebergs found?	**Temperature**	30
How much does the heaviest fruit weigh?	**Fruit**	32
Why do plants and animals have to be protected?	**Conservation**	34
How long do trees live?	**Trees**	36
Which are the largest birds?	**Birds**	38
How fast can fish swim?	**Fish**	40
Which is older, man or beast?	**Dinosaurs**	42
How big do snakes grow?	**Reptiles**	44
Which plants and animals are poisonous?	**Poison**	46
How much can insects carry?	**Insects**	48
How much does a person need to eat?	**Nutrition**	50
Who has the best tastebuds?	**Taste**	52
Who has the best hearing?	**Hearing**	54
Do animals kiss each other?	**Behavior**	56
When were the greatest inventions?	**Inventions**	58
What has the greatest mass?	**Mass**	60
How many people will there be in 2000 AD?	**Population**	62
Who has what?	**Rich and poor**	64
How much can a child carry?	**Gravity**	66
How many noughts in 10^{12}?	**Counting systems**	68
What has the best eyesight?	**Eyes**	70
How big is a foot?	**Measurements**	72
Highest mountains and deepest depths	**Mountains and valleys**	74
How fast can a snail travel?	**Speed**	76
Who gets up first?	**Time zones**	78
How long is the shortest year?	**Calendar**	80
What can carry the most passengers?	**Transport**	82
How big is a soccer pitch?	**Sports**	84
Where is the longest bridge?	**Bridges and tunnels**	86

How hot is it at the equator?	**Temperature**	88
How big is the Earth?	**Distances**	90
Wonders of the world	**Some records**	92
Which countries are most populated?	**Population**	94
How big is North America?	**Geographic facts**	96
Which is the biggest country in Europe?	**Europe**	98
Which is the biggest continent?	**Continents**	100
Which is the biggest island?	**Islands**	102
Warm or cold-blooded?	**Body temperature**	104
Is the sun the largest planet?	**Volume**	106
How much water can an oil tanker hold?	**Volume**	108
Who uses the most energy?	**Energy**	110
Which is the greatest source of energy?	**Energy**	112
How heavy is flyweight?	**Weight**	114
Who can move fastest in water?	**Speed**	116
How long is a year?	**Seasons**	118
Which is the most accurate clock?	**Time measurements**	120
Which is the biggest river in the world?	**Rivers**	122

125